Anne of the Thousand Days: The Making of an Epic

By

Jennifer K. Lafferty

Copyright © 2019 by Jennifer Lafferty
All Rights Reserved

Cover Photograph: Publicity photo of Geneviève Bujold for *Anne of the Thousand Days*, movie studio [public domain]

For Reagan with love

Contents

"The King's Great Matter" Plays Out on the Big Screen

Based on Historical Events

Henry and Anne Hold Court on Broadway

Hal B. Wallis A.K.A. The Starmaker

From Stage Play to Screenplay

Richard Burton as Henry VIII

Geneviève Bujold as Anne Boleyn

An Impressive Cast of Supporting Players

Directing History: Charles Jarrott

New Friendships and Old Rivalries

Reports from the Set

Henry & Anne & Richard & Geneviève

Dressing Up

Georges Delerue's Haunting Soundtrack

World Premiere and Awards Season

Fact Vs. Fiction

Anne Boleyn as a Pop Culture Icon

"The King's Great Matter" Plays Out on the Big Screen

Occasionally, we will see a motion picture depiction of historical events that is so compelling or vivid or inspiring, it replaces the long held ideas viewers previously had of the story and the real historical figures. Watching *Anne of the Thousand Days*, it is easy to see how this can happen.

This 1969 Hal B. Wallis epic, starring Geneviève Bujold and Richard Burton was not the first cinematic adaptation of what was known in the early 16th century as "The King's Great Matter", and certainly wasn't the last, but it has stood out as the quintessential version for the past 50 years.

It is natural to be swept away by this tragically romantic, aesthetically beautiful and brilliantly acted saga. The movie is entertaining on multiple levels. It is almost satirical in places, which is not that uncommon in melodramas. It's tempting to believe that the humorous moments are intentional, but regardless of how the irony and campiness came about, it is useful in helping to keep the film from becoming too heavy, early on.

The plan to adapt *Anne of the Thousand Days* was first hatched by Wallis while he was filming the popular Richard Burton-Peter O'Toole historical drama *Becket*, in 1962. Wallis would later compare the two films, while pointing out that *Anne* was on a grander emotional scale. It would take seven years for *Anne of the Thousand Days* to reach fruition.

One reason it took so long is because the material was considered too provocative for the cinema at the time. Additionally, Wallis, who was known for his flawless taste and high quality productions, was not willing to compromise when it came to casting or the scale of the project. He embarked on a search for the perfect actress to play Anne Boleyn, which led him to exciting newcomer Geneviève Bujold. He was intent on getting Richard Burton, despite having to wait until the busy actor could make time in his schedule.

The passage of time factors largely into how this piece of 2h 26m celluloid artistry is capable of overshadowing history itself. These events took place over four hundred years earlier; before photography or recorded sound or modern journalism.

For a long time, impressions of the famous king and his ill-fated queen tended to be sketchy and one dimensional, especially those that were filtered down to the general public. Except for a few historical scholars, most people viewed Henry VIII as a chauvinistic, obese, hot-headed tyrant, whose insatiable lust for Anne, presumed to be a calculating temptress, drove him to forsake his wife, despite consequences of monumental proportions, resulting in England's break with the Roman Catholic Church.

It's not that any of this is patently false, there's just so much more to it. Hal Wallis' film adaptation of Maxwell Anderson's hit play fleshed out the characters and explored the complexity of the story.

We see a different version of Henry; one who can often seem very human, even sensitive at times, and an Anne who can be vulnerable and tender. There are moments when it's possible to actually relate to these people and find things about them to admire. Their love for one another, although fleeting, seems real.

While watching the romance play out, we can almost forget that the tale has a very sad and gruesome ending.

It is an impressive feat that the filmmakers and actors were able to so successfully shift the focus away from Anne's well-known execution, ordered by Henry, especially since this is what we remember most about their relationship.

It is necessary for the audience to stay in the moment, because we are seeing events through the eyes of Henry, Anne and other characters who had no idea how things would turn out, at least not until Henry made up his mind to get rid of this woman, who just a few years before, he could not live without.

Based on Historical Events

The true story of Henry VIII, Anne Boleyn and the lasting impact their relationship had on the world has inspired countless writers over the past five hundred years. Although many of these authors have taken liberties and spun fictionalized accounts of what took place at the Tudor court during this enthralling chapter of history, the real historical events hardly need embellishment to fascinate any reader, theater or moviegoer.

This raw material has, and will probably always, inspire creative retellings, but Maxwell Anderson's play *Anne of the Thousand Days* and its film adaptation remain among the very best so far.

The perfect storm that led to Henry VIII's break with the Roman Catholic Church and prompted the English Reformation really began in the early 1520s when a charming teenaged Anne Boleyn, the daughter of the prominent diplomat/politician Thomas Boleyn and Elizabeth Boleyn née Howard (daughter of the Duke of Norfolk), returned to the English court from a lengthy stay in Europe, mainly France, and soon acquired a number of male admirers. Within the next couple of years, the king himself, would be among them.

During the time she had spent serving Queen Claude, wife of the French king Francis I, Anne became cultured, sophisticated and attained noticeably French ways, which would initially increase her appeal but later hasten her downfall.

Surrounded by courtesans vying for his favor, Henry, who had already taken her older sister Mary as a lover, was struck by Anne, who he observed to be very unique. But it was not only because she was a Francophile that Anne appeared exotic.

Anne possessed the gifts of wit, cleverness and superior intellect. The fact that she showed off these qualities and seemed so self-assured, instead of cloaking herself in modesty and humility as women of this time were expected to do, caused many to take a critical view of her. The higher Anne rose in the King's favor, the more enemies she made and this was due, at least in part, to her arrogance.

It was becoming increasingly clear that Henry's queen consort, the reserved, dutiful Katherine of Aragon, in many ways Anne Boleyn's polar opposite, was not going to give birth to a healthy male heir.

The many attempts over the years had produced several stillborn infants and babies who had not lived long. Queen Katherine was nearing the end of her childbearing years and the couple's only surviving child was Princess Mary, who was largely seen as unfit to rule, by virtue of the fact that she was a girl.

No one, it would seem, was more against the idea of a female, one day, leading the nation than Henry, who was desperate to father a healthy, legitimate male heir, but in order to do that he would have to dissolve his marriage to Katherine.

Either deeply infatuated with or in love with Anne, the king ordered Cardinal Wolsey to deny permission for her to marry Lord Henry Percy. The proposed union was apparently not a typical arranged marriage, so common among the nobility of that era, but a love match.

Naturally, Anne was upset about being forbidden to marry the man she loved, but she was also very ambitious and in time, came around to the idea of a romantic relationship with Henry, although, unlike her sister Mary, she was not content to be the king's mistress. She reportedly refused to consummate their relationship for several years, at least until it became very clear that Henry was determined to free himself of Katherine in order to wed Anne and make her his queen.

Henry's strategy to get rid of Katherine, so that he could marry Anne, was to argue that his marriage to Katherine should be annulled, on the grounds that it was incest in the eyes of God, because she had previously been married to his elder brother Arthur. This is an aspect of the story that was mentioned in the film but the full account is very interesting.

The Spanish-born Katherine of Aragon was the daughter of Ferdinand II of Aragon and Isabella I of Castile (yes, the same Queen Isabella who sponsored Columbus' voyage, which resulted in his discovery of America).

At the age of 16, Katherine was sent to England to marry the 15-year-old Arthur, Prince of Wales, in order to form a political alliance between England and Spain.

It was a marriage that Arthur's parents Henry Tudor and his queen Elizabeth of York very much wanted, but Isabella and Ferdinand had hesitated due to King Henry's much contested claim to the throne. However, they eventually acquiesced and the young couple was married on November 14, 1501.

Katherine would later claim that the marriage was never consummated, contrary to assumptions at the time that the teenagers had bedded, which was reinforced by a bawdy remark Arthur had made the morning after their wedding.

When Arthur became ill, likely from a virus known as the "sweating sickness" and died just five months after the wedding, the question of whether or not the marriage had been consummated became very important. Since Arthur died without issue, his brother, the not quite 11-year-old Henry was, now heir to the throne, and his father was anxious to keep the alliance with Spain, so he arranged for Henry to marry Katherine several years later.

Because Katherine was the widow of his brother, this required a dispensation from the Pope, which was granted based on the belief that her marriage to Arthur had not been consummated. This cleared the path for Henry and Katherine to wed on June 11, 1509, less than two months after Henry ascended the throne, following his father's death.

Despite the difference in their ages and the contrast in their personalities, the serious-minded Katherine and playful Henry appeared to have a relatively good relationship. In the first decade of their marriage, Katherine gave birth to at least six babies, including two, much hoped for boys. However, all of these children, with the exception of their daughter Mary, were either stillborn or died as infants.

Chauvinistic as he could be in some areas, Henry seemed to like intelligence in a woman. Anne Boleyn, like Katherine of Aragon, possessed a superior intellect which the king found stimulating. It was probably a combination of her brains, charm, charisma, sophistication, and youth that drew Henry to Anne so strongly, during this anxious time, when the hope of Katherine bearing a healthy male heir was quickly diminishing.

Some argue that Henry was not the lecher, that we have read about and seen depicted in films for so long, and that he had few affairs during all the years he was married to Katherine. If this is true, it adds validity to the theory that his feelings for Anne were more than mere lust. However, his attraction, or even love for Anne, was clearly not his only motivation for seeking an annulment. Henry now had what seemed to him, a good excuse for throwing over Katherine for a new bride, the "necessity" for a male heir to rule his kingdom one day.

Henry is also seen as fickle when it comes to women, an automatic assumption when one finds out that he had six wives; and while this was probably true to some extent it should be remembered that most of his marriages ended for other reasons.

During Henry's first two marriages he was focused on conceiving a healthy male heir, which did not happen. His third wife, Jane Seymour, died within days of childbirth. He disliked his fourth wife, Anne of Cleves, whom he married for a political alliance, from the beginning and ended the marriage six months later. Wife no. 5, the much younger Katherine Howard, was executed after she was convicted of treason on the grounds of adultery, like her cousin Anne Boleyn. But the claims of Katherine's alleged infidelity are viewed as more credible than those made against Anne. Charges were also brought against Katherine because she failed to disclose her sexual history prior to marrying the king. Henry's last wife, Katherine Parr, survived him.

Although he did eventually tire of Anne, she managed to hold his interest for at least seven years leading up to their marriage, which lasted for three years. Watching *Anne of the Thousand Days* we do not get a sense of how long Henry and Anne's relationship lasted, which included the six years that Henry spent attempting to convince the Pope to annul his marriage to Katherine so that he could wed Anne, or the full complexity of this struggle and the subsequent Reformation.

Of course, *Anne of the Thousand Days*, is not a documentary, but a glamorous, somewhat fictionalized feature film, which according to its producer Hal B. Wallis, is mainly a love story. Obviously, it was necessary to condense much of the history because of time restraints. But for the sake of perspective it is important for us to understand that Henry and Anne had a lengthy romance and that it was based on more than infatuation. It should also be pointed out that, unlike some dramatizations, *Anne of the Thousand Days* did not explore Anne Boleyn's interest in religion and her support of the early Reformation. Not only was this an important part of the character but her ideology is thought to have had a significant influence on Henry's views as well.

The basis for Henry's annulment case was a Biblical passage in Leviticus, forbidding a marriage between a man and his brother's widow. It also warns that such a union will be childless, a convenient explanation for why Henry and Katherine's marriage had produced no surviving male heirs, which would also help to counteract any 16th century suspicions that a lack of virility on Henry's part might be to blame for the problem. Henry maintained that Katherine had lied when she said her marriage to Arthur was never consummated.

Pope Clement VII was extremely reluctant to even consider granting the dispensation Henry needed, presumably, because he did not want to alienate Katherine's own nephew, Charles V, who was both the king of Spain and the Holy Roman Emperor.

The Pope finally allowed Henry to try the case before a papal commission and sent Cardinal Campeggio, who was the "protector of England" in the Roman Curia. When it became obvious that the Pope was not going to grant the dispensation, Henry decided to take matters into his own hands.

Angry over Cardinal Wolsey's failed efforts to negotiate with Rome, Henry discharged him as chancellor in 1529, replacing him with Sir Thomas More, who would only agree to take the job if he didn't have to be involved in the divorce. Wolsey would be arrested in November of 1530 and charged with treason but died a few weeks later, after becoming ill in route to London, to answer the charges against him. In 1531 Henry separated from Katherine and appointed lawyer/politician Thomas Cromwell to the inner circle of his council. Soon thereafter he followed Cromwell's advice to break with the Roman Church. Henry was later ex-communicated for this action.

Although it is believed that Anne and Henry did not consummate their relationship until they traveled to France together in the autumn of 1532, by then the two had been living in close proximity for sometime, and he had made her Marquise of Pembroke.

Henry and Anne did not marry until it was discovered that she was pregnant. The couple wed secretly on January 25, 1533. After years of waiting and wondering, things were suddenly happening very quickly. Henry's marriage to Katherine was declared void in a court assembled by reformist Thomas Cranmer, who had recently been appointed Archbishop of Canterbury. A few days later Cranmer proclaimed the king's marriage to Anne was valid, following a special inquiry.

Anne was crowned Queen on the third day of her coronation festivities, June 1, 1533. Katherine was demoted to Dowager Princess of Wales. Princess Mary was now considered illegitimate as a result of the annulment, meaning she was no longer next in line to the throne. Henry and Anne's, baby the future Queen Elizabeth I, born September 7, 1533, was the new heir presumptive.

The birth of Princess Elizabeth was a disappointment after the lengths Henry had gone to in order to try to get a legitimate male heir. However, Anne and Henry's reaction to the birth of a daughter instead of a son was likely exaggerated, when depicted in novels and in films like *Anne of the Thousand Days*. Henry seemed to take pride in little Elizabeth, showing her off at court. As some historians point out, the proof that Anne was capable of delivering a healthy child would have been a relief and given the couple hope for the future.

We tend to zero in on Anne's failure to produce a male heir, -- first giving birth to a girl and then suffering multiple miscarriages -- as the reason for her downfall, which led to her execution. It was more likely a combination of this and the strife that arose from her jealousy over the attention Henry was paying to other women, the embarrassment caused by her public outbursts, and the efforts of ally-turned enemy, Cromwell, to destroy her.

Both of them being reformists, Anne Boleyn and Thomas Cromwell were once united in a common goal. Cromwell helped Anne get to the throne but ironically, he was probably the person most responsible for her demise.

After Anne became queen, she and Cromwell were soon at odds. There were heated public arguments and Anne tried to persuade Henry against taking Cromwell's advise on matters of policy, notably the issue of how to distribute the financial spoils of the debunked monasteries. Cromwell wanted the money to go to the crown, while Anne argued it should be given to charities.

Anne was also quite brazen in her attacks on Cromwell, famously ordering a church sermon to be given on Passion Sunday 1536, in which her almoner John Skip stressed the importance of the King finding wisdom within himself instead of listening to "evil councilors"; and talked about Haman, of the Old Testament, enemy of Queen Esther, who attempted to send riches to the royal treasury, which were taken from Jews, who he had persecuted. At the end of the story Haman is headed to his death on the scaffold.

Like many, before and after her, it could be said that Anne's arrogance was really her undoing. It seems that she overestimated her own power, while underestimating what Cromwell was capable of doing. This is somewhat surprising, considering Anne's cleverness and sophistication. But a sense of her own importance as queen consort of England may have blinded her to the dangers of antagonizing someone like Cromwell. This brings to mind the oft repeated modern expression: *I made you and I can break you*, which to a large extent is what Cromwell did with Anne Boleyn.

In *Anne of the Thousand Days*, we do not see these motivations Cromwell almost certainly had for wanting to get rid of Anne. In the movie, he appears to be an ambitious man, which he indeed was, whose goal is to please the king, presumably to ultimately further his own interests.

The sort of palace intrigue that occurred in real life is fascinating and informative, but while it would fit well into another type of film, isn't really necessary in the context of a romantic melodrama like *Anne of the Thousand Days*, any more than it is in the opera *Anna Bolena*, which shows Henry ousting Anne almost entirely due to his burning passion for Jane Seymour. Although Henry VIII's court could sometimes resemble an opera or a melodrama, at the end of the day everything boiled down to politics.

Cromwell was so determined to defeat the Queen he joined forces with his enemies, who were now plotting against Anne, a group of conservatives, whose ideology was in opposition to his own. Among this group were the Seymour Brothers, whose sister, Jane, was already being thought of as an agreeable replacement for Anne.

It would have looked absurd to use an excuse based on some religious conflict to cast out Anne, considering the long, hard battle that Henry had recently fought with Rome, in trying to annul his marriage to Katherine, on similar grounds. Instead, Cromwell used the damning allegation of treason.

In late April, Cromwell left court for a week, probably to map out his strategy to take down Anne once and for all. He would use her flirtatious behavior, which had helped her win the favor of the King himself, and her habit of surrounding herself with male admirers, as ammunition against her in order to make the case that she had committed adultery.

Cromwell investigated Anne's conduct and may, according to some sources, have twisted the words or even bribed witnesses for his own purposes and then presented the information to the King. There is a difference of opinion among historians as to whether or not Henry was immediately convinced. Some say he instructed Cromwell to amass all the evidence necessary for a conviction while others argue that he was not so quick to turn his back on Anne.

There is every reason to believe Cromwell was the architect of Anne's downfall. Besides his obvious and powerful motives, Spanish ambassador Eustace Chapuys, who was one of Anne's biggest critics, said Cromwell was the one responsible for what happened. Additionally, it is probably not a coincidence that most of the men dragged into the scandal, were Cromwell's political adversaries and he arranged for two of his friends who were arrested, to be released.

Anne's musician Mark Smeaton was invited to Cromwell's house where, according to rumor, a confession was tortured out of him, and he provided the names of others. Some of the men charged were among Henry's closest friends, such as Henry Norris, who was offered a pardon in exchange for a confession.

Anne was taken more or less off guard, though she did at least have an inkling that something was amiss, having a conversation with her chaplain Matthew Park on April 26, in which she asked him to take care of Elizabeth if anything happened to her. The day after attending a May Day celebration with the King, during which he had abruptly walked out after receiving a note, Anne was arrested and imprisoned in the Tower of London, along with her brother George who was accused of committing incest with her.

The Queen's trial seems to have been a mockery of justice. The evidence against her was based on gossip and misinterpretation of courtly behavior. It's obvious to today's scholars that the judges were Henry's puppets, and many of his actions just prior to the trial strongly indicate he had no doubt she would be convicted.

Anne's intelligence, wisdom and caginess were reflected in the careful way she responded to questioning at her trial. She displayed remarkable grace under fire as she calmly denied the charges against her, but once she was taken back to the Tower after she had been sentenced to death for high treason, Anne snapped and became hysterical.

Cromwell remained vigilant during Anne's imprisonment, sending spies to the tower and having Constable, Sir William Kingston, report to him on her conduct. Something a nervous Anne admitted to Kingston, soon after being taken to the Tower, might have actually incriminated her the most. She recalled a recent flirtatious chat she'd had with Henry Norris, in which she teased him about his constant presence in the King's chamber, joking that he was waiting for Henry to die so he could have her to himself.

This sort of repartee might sound shocking to us, but at a 16th century court, where spirited flirtation was encouraged and even expected, such words wouldn't have seemed so outrageous, at least not ordinarily. But considering the suspicion she was under, provocative banter like this definitely could have made the charges against her seem more credible.

At one point, Anne wrote a letter to Henry. The elegant, articulate letter, seems to have been composed with a cool, clear head, similar to the speech she gave at her trial just after being sentenced. However, Anne is adamant in proclaiming her innocence, and she lambaste Henry for his cruelty, reminding him he will soon enough have to account for his behavior before God on judgment day. She beseeches him to believe she was a faithful wife and that if he is unwilling to spare her, to at least refrain from condemning the innocent men who were accused with her. It is unknown whether the letter failed to change the king's mind or if he never actually saw it, since it was found among Cromwell's papers.

On May 17, 1536 George Boleyn, Sir Henry Norris, Sir William Brereton, Sir Francis Weston, and Mark Smeaton, the five men found guilty of adultery with the Queen and convicted of high treason, were executed. Anne Boleyn was beheaded at the Tower of London on May 19, 1536. Cromwell, who was in attendance at the execution, soon made an ally of Jane Seymour, who Henry quickly married following Anne's execution

Henry and Anne Hold Court on Broadway

Long before *Anne of the Thousand Days* hit the big screen, it started life in Broadway's Shubert Theatre, December 8, 1948, as a romantic drama penned by Maxwell Anderson and staged by H.C. Potter. In this memorable season which included the premiers of such classics as: *South Pacific, Kiss Me, Kate,* and *Death of a Salesman*, this historical play, set in Tudor England, from 1526-1536, held its own, running for 288 performances over 10 months -- with a 2-month hiatus -- and earned two Tony awards.

The subject of 16th century British royals was a familiar one for accomplished playwright/producer/lyricist Maxwell Anderson, who had written the Broadway drama *Elizabeth the Queen*, which was made into the 1939 Hal B. Wallis film *The Private Lives of Elizabeth and Essex,* starring Bette Davis. His *Mary of Scotland* was also adapted to the big screen for the 1936 Katharine Hepburn film by the same name.

By the early 20th century Maxwell Anderson, who was born in Atlantic, Pennsylvania December 15, 1888, had already become one of the most prominent playwrights around. When he was a boy, Anderson and his family moved frequently, due his father's occupation as a traveling Baptist minister.

Anderson did not immediately focus his energy on writing for the theater when he graduated from college -- earning his bachelors degree from the University of North Dakota in 1911 and an M.A. from Stanford in 1914 – but chose to work as an educator for several years.

He then went on to write for a number of newspapers, including the *San Francisco Chronicle* and *The New York Globe*, eventually becoming an editorial writer for liberal magazine *The New Republic*. He also founded the magazine *The Measure: A Journal of Poetry* in 1921. Politics and war are subjects that can frequently be found in Anderson's work, including *Anne of the Thousand Days*, which is full of political intrigue and maneuvering, as well as the looming threat of war with Spain and English civil war.

While his politically themed plays, like the Pulitzer-winning *Both Your Houses* often received accolades, political statements could be very detrimental to his other occupations. Pro-Pacifist remarks he made to students, while he was a high school principal in Minnewaukan, North Dakota, apparently led to Anderson losing his job. Similar statements, a few years later, cost him his job as chairman of the English department at Whittier College.

It was likely a combination of Anderson's unconventional leanings and his love of poetry that resulted in his decision to write many plays in blank verse. One of his objectives was also to write about people who live according to their beliefs despite the power of evil in the world around them. This is a theme that is at least touched on in *Anne of the Thousand Days*, when we see the execution of statesman Thomas More for refusing to acknowledge Henry as the head of the Church of England because it goes against his beliefs. At times even Henry, himself, is depicted as struggling with his conscience and fervently praying for forgiveness.

Another factor that probably drew Anderson to the story of Anne Boleyn was his keenness for tragedy. There was plenty of drama and tragedy in Anderson's personal life as well. *Anne of the Thousand Days* largely focuses on infidelity and Henry's habit of jumping from one relationship to another; two things Maxwell Anderson would have understood from personal experience.

Anderson was married the first time in 1911, to college sweetheart Margaret Haskett. The couple had three sons together but they separated in 1931, after he began an affair with the married actress Gertrude Higger "Mab Anthony". Although it has been widely reported that they where married in 1933, following Haskett's death, Anderson's daughter with Higger, Hesper Anderson, claimed that she discovered the two were never married.

Decadence and more infidelity damaged Anderson and Higger's relationship, which ended when he left her in 1953, shortly after which Higger committed suicide. Anderson finally found real happiness with his last wife, former actress Gilda Hazard, who he was married to from 1954 until his death in 1959. Hazard also provided the encouragement Anderson, who was in ill heath at the time, needed to write his last big hit for the stage, *The Bad Seed*, adapted from William March's novel.

Hesper Anderson discusses the troubled atmosphere of her childhood in her sensitive memoir *South Mountain Road: A Daughter's Journey of Discovery*, which also sheds light on her father's difficult childhood. Maxwell Anderson's own autobiographical book, *Morning, Winter and Night* – written under a pseudonym – explores an abusive childhood. Therefore it is not at all surprising that the playwright would gravitate toward turbulent and sad material. However, he occasionally tried his hand at romantic comedy but it was his dramatic stage plays and screenplays for which he is best remembered.

One of his most valuable contributions to the theater was the realization of his dream to bring poetic drama back to the stage, succeeding, as his biographer Alfred S. Shivers points out, with such plays as the highly praised *Winterset*.

His eldest son, Quentin, carved out an impressive niche. In addition to being a professor at Columbia University, Quentin made a name for himself as a critic, cultural historian and author.

Anne of the Thousand Days was produced by The Playwrights' Company and legendary Hollywood agent-turned film and stage producer Leland Hayward. Earlier in the year Hayward's hit play *Mister Roberts* had premiered on Broadway. His most iconic shows, including *Gypsy* and *The Sound of Music*, were still ahead.

The prologue of the first act has Anne in the Tower of London awaiting her execution which she is still not certain will occur. She is reflecting on her life with Henry, as she does at the start of the famous Tower scene toward the end of the film adaptation. Unlike the film, the opening of the play firmly establishes Anne as a combination of a victim and villain. She looks back on the part she played in having men unjustly executed and sees that she may be about to suffer the same fate she inflicted on others. Circling back to the life she shared with Henry, she grapples with the idea that he may actually put her to death, obviously finding the notion difficult to accept. She can't reconcile the image of him in her mind with his role as her would be executioner. She acknowledges how things have changed between them and asks herself if she would be capable of killing him. Admitting to herself that maybe she would be able to have Henry killed, if things were reversed, she reasons that perhaps he can kill her.

Her speech provides important insight into the relationship of Henry and Anne as well as the makeup of their individual characters. It sets the tone for what is to follow, as opposed to the film, which allows the viewer to make these discoveries gradually and gives us more freedom to interpret the characters as we wish.

One of the most striking differences between *Anne of the Thousand Days* theatrical and the cinematic version is that the play spends significantly more time exploring the feelings of the characters and in revealing the various backstories. Since plays are often considerably longer and more drawn out than movies, this is a luxury stage productions can afford. Dialogue is also relied on more heavily in plays to convey emotions, perspectives and opinions that can be communicated on film, with fewer words and effective close-up or clever editing.

The play examines how Anne's influence on Henry went beyond the passion she stirred in him, and on the impact she had on court life. It delves more deeply into Henry's soul and possible motives for his actions.

Max Anderson so skillfully fleshed out the characters with his thoughtful and illuminating dialogue that there is less of a burden on the actors and director, than there is on those who worked on a film adaptation of the story, to create these complex full bodied characters.

The Henry VIII of Maxwell Anderson's play was a notably tragic figure when compared with the popular perception of him at the time as a jolly, gluttonous fiend, which Charles Laughton had captured so vividly in *The Private Lives of Henry VIII* more than 15 years earlier. Anderson's Henry, who can be very serious and reflective is a man who, at the end of the play, broods over the consequences of England's break with Rome and who knows he will be forever haunted by the memory of Anne, his great love, after she is gone.

In addition to its other merits, *Anne of the Thousand Days* is a great acting vehicle. For those who did not get the opportunity to see Rex Harrison's Tony winning portrayal of Henry VIII but who have seen Richard Burton's performance, it is difficult to imagine Harrison's interpretation; and that two actors with such different styles could have each been so successful in the role.

Burton naturally brought a romantic quality to most of his performances, including, to some extent, Henry. He played him as a passionate suitor. We see Henry VIII not just in lust but in love. *Could such a thing be possible*? we ask ourselves, but the actor is clever enough to convince us it's true, at least until the spell is broken when the movie comes to an end. However, Harrison rarely came across as romantic, even while starring as the male love interest in romantic films. He could be charming and had a sophisticated sex appeal, but the part of an ardent lover was not his forte.

One thing he did have in common with Burton was his skill for playing high-born men, frequently being cast as aristocrats or royalty. Harrison had an easy elegance and regality in his demeanor that made him a natural for such roles.

Rex Harrison, born in Huyton, Lancashire, England in 1908 as Reginald Carey Harrison, is perhaps best remembered for playing the awkward, unlikely suitor, such as Henry Higgins in *My Fair Lady* and Captain Gregg in *The Ghost and Mrs. Muir*. His bold, arrogant persona was in keeping with the image of King Henry shaped by Charles Laughton and others over the years. Like the real Henry VIII, Harrison had a reputation for a roving eye and was married six times. Both of his sons, Noel, (with first wife Collette Thomas) and Carey, (with second wife and frequent co-star Lilli Palmer) became actors.

Like so many actors of his generation, Harrison started out in the theater and then transitioned into film but, stage struck as he was from an early age, he actually joined a repertory company when he was just 16-years-old and had the opportunity to hone his craft for years before making his first film in 1930 with the picture *The Great Game*, and debuting on the London stage the same year.

Harrison amassed an impressive resume over the next 18 years, starring in popular movies like *Blithe Spirit*, *Night Train to Munich* and *Anna and the King of Siam*, as well as plays like Noël Coward's *Design for Living*, before starring in the original Broadway production of *Anne of the Thousand Days*.

Joyce Redman began her Broadway run in the title role of Maxwell Anderson's play the day before her 33rd birthday. By the time she stepped into the shoes of the intriguingly complex Anne Boleyn, Redman, who trained at the Royal Academy of Dramatic Art, had already established herself on London's West End and joined the legendary Old Vic company in 1944.

Early on, the spirited, petite redhead, with a husky voice, proved herself capable of tackling a wide range of genres from Shakespearian tragedy like Olivier's *Richard III* to light-hearted fantasy like *Peter Pan*, but hadn't yet conquered Broadway. She did enjoy notable success in the UK. Her most impressive performance prior to her interpretation of Anne Boleyn, was likely her critically acclaimed Cordelia in Olivier's *King Lear* (1946). However, since debuting on the Great White Way in 1946 as Doll Tearsheet in a revival of *Henry IV Part II*, she had mainly played small parts in repertory and short-lived productions.

Redman, who was born in Newcastle, Northumberland, England to a British father and Irish mother, grew up in County Mayo, Ireland. She began her screen career in 1938, appearing in a smattering of supporting roles over the next decade. While her movie and TV career was more impressive following *Anne of the Thousand Days*, her most memorable role being the lusty Mrs. Waters in the 1963 sex romp *Tom Jones*, her time starring as Anne was one of the biggest highlights of her career, just as it was for her successor, Geneviève Bujold, 20 years later.

Redman married Charles Wynne-Roberts, a former British army captain, soon after *Anne* premiered and the couple had three children, including actor Crispin Redman.

Redman resembled the real Anne in some respects, including her saucer eyes – although hers were blue -- and prominent nose. She had a strikingly attractive face, like Geneviève Bujold, but the two women were different types physically, except for their short stature which, ironically, differed from Anne Boleyn, who was taller than average. Something else Redman had in common with Geneviève was her ability to deliver a fiery, and at times, sensual performance, which is essential for any actress playing Anderson's version of Anne Boleyn.

In the role of Anne Boleyn's fiancé, Percy, Earl of Northumberland, was the dashing actor Robert Duke, whose career was filled with historical and Shakespearian drama. Shortly before appearing in *Anne*, Duke had played a supporting character in *Antony and Cleopatra*. His next Broadway role would be Paris, in a production of *Romeo and Juliet*.

Playing Anne's father, Thomas Boleyn, was Broadway veteran Charles Francis, who had been acting in the theater for more than 35 years. His resume spans a wide range of genres including Shakespeare, mystery, comedy, musicals and classical drama.

Russell Gaige, who played Thomas More, had little experience on the stage before coming to this role. He had just started in the theater in 1945. His most notable role prior to *Anne* was as Doctor Chambers in a short-lived run of the comedy revival *The Barretts of Wimpole Street*.

Mary Boleyn, who was Anne's sister and the king's discarded mistress, was played by Louise Platt, who had appeared in five Broadway plays from 1936 through 1941. *Anne of the Thousand Days* marked her return to Broadway theater after a seven year absence. All of her previous plays had very brief runs. *Anne* was her first and only hit. From March 31 to May 28, 1949, Platt was also performing in a melodrama titled *The Traitor*, which was produced by her husband, Jed Harris. When *Anne* went on hiatus on June 26, 1949, Platt left the play and did not return when it reopened on August 21.

One of the most prominent supporting actors in *Anne* was the 68-year-old British-born Percy Waram who portrayed the key figure of Cardinal Wolsey. Waram had many impressive credits during his long career on the New York stage, spanning the years 1903-1957. He had played Sir Walter Raleigh in Maxwell Anderson's *Elizabeth the Queen*, which premiered in 1930. Other highlights include a starring turn as Roger Newcombe in *The Late George Apley* 1944-45, the original 1935 Broadway production of *Pride and Prejudice*, in which he played Mr. Bennet, and his role as the judge in *The Chalk Garden* (1955-56). Waram also left *Anne* permanently when the production went on hiatus.

Wendell K. Phillips played one of the most interesting roles in *Anne of the Thousand Days*, the cagey Thomas Cromwell. Phillips, who was also a producer, director and designer, had been performing on Broadway for nearly 25 years when *Anne* premiered. His most notable plays included *Waiting for Lefty* in 1935 and *Many Mansions* 1937-38.

With a period drama taking place at a royal court, elements such as set and costume design are particularly important. Jo Mielziner would win a Tony for the play's set design but his original elaborate sets had to be scrapped and rebuilt during the middle of rehearsals.

The book *Design by Motley* recounts the challenges Motley designer Elizabeth Montgomery faced working on this play. The fact that Rex Harrison was such a different type physically from the image we have of Henry VIII, based on the Holbein cartoons and portraits of the king in his later years, presented some difficulty for Motley, assuming that a hefty actor would be cast. Eventually special beefy legs that cost $1,000 had to be made in Hollywood for Harrison to disguise his own skinny legs. Harrison's chest and shoulders were also padded. Another trick that was used to make him appear larger was narrow doorways on the set.

The play dictated that Henry appear in a wide range of costumes, including sporting clothes, court dress and casual clothing. Elizabeth Montgomery found inspiration in paintings and descriptions of Tudor costume. Harrison and Redman had 28 costume changes. In order for the changes to be done quickly, the designer made a device that could snap the costumes on or off. The change for the coronation scene only took 30 seconds.

This original Broadway production of *Anne of the Thousand Days* closed on October 8, 1949. There would be multiple revivals of the play, including several during the first two decades of the 2000s.

Hal B. Wallis, already a powerful Hollywood producer at the time, saw *Anne of the Thousand Days* in 1949 and appreciated it, but while this is the sort of project that easily lends itself to the big screen, it would take 20 years for the production to commence on his epic film adaptation.

Hal B. Wallis A.K.A. The Starmaker

It's surprising to learn that the same hard-boiled, straight-talking pragmatist who first made a name for himself producing gangster films in the 1930s, was also the driving force responsible for bringing *Anne of the Thousand Days* to the big screen. While Hal Wallis scored many hits with earthy action-adventure pics, he had a versatile repertoire and wide ranging taste. Some of the greatest films he produced were melodramas like *Now Voyager*, and one of the most popular romances of all time, *Casablanca*.

Hal Wallis was a true Anglophile, in love with British culture. A self-taught scholar of British history, beginning in his childhood, Hal was anxious to share stories of Britain's fascinating past with moviegoers. It must have been very gratifying when Queen Elizabeth II was so impressed by his efforts after a Royal Command Performance of *Anne of the Thousand Days*, she told him that his films were teaching them about English history, and honored him with the title Commander of the British Empire a few years later.

Wallis' first serious attempt to adapt British history to the big screen was *The Private Lives of Elizabeth and Essex*, released in 1939. Two decades later he still had a taste for historical drama and was sure moviegoers did too, even though friends and associates tried to persuade him otherwise. He was determined to make the play *Becket* into a film despite insistence from Paramount executives that the story, focusing on the monumental church-state clash between former friends Archbishop of Canterbury Thomas Becket and King Henry II, was not commercially viable at the time. He talked Paramount into letting him do the film by explaining that he would dress it up with beautiful costumes and locations, as he would later do with *Anne of the Thousand Days*.

Nominated for a dozen Oscars, the highly acclaimed *Becket* (1964) starring Peter O'Toole as the debaucherous Henry II and Richard Burton as his friend-turned adversary Thomas Becket, prompted Wallis to further indulge his interest in British history with a series of historic epics that included *Anne of the Thousand Days* and *Mary, Queen of Scots*.

Throughout his 1980 memoir, *Starmaker: The Autobiography of Hal Wallis*, there are indications that he was preoccupied with money but of course, frugality is an almost essential trait for a film producer to have. If he was overly concerned with finances it was probably due, in no small part, to the hardships of his childhood and lack of financial security that made it necessary for him to go to work at a very early age to help support his family.

Harold Brent Wallis was born in Chicago on September 14, 1899 to a Polish mother and Russian father who were both Jewish immigrants. Hal had two older sisters, Minna, who would eventually become one of the most powerful agents in Hollywood, and Juel who married screenwriter Wally Kline.

Their father, who worked as a tailor, gambled away his modest salary and the Wallis' continually struggled to pay the bills. Their father walked out on the family when Hal was a teenager and it was during this time frame that they were in such bad shape financially he had to leave school at 14-years-old to get a job as an office boy. All three of the Wallis children worked to support the family and Hal, who was forced to grow up fast, had to shoulder much responsibility at an early age.

An ambitious go-getter from the outset, the young Hal Wallis soon distinguished himself as a top salesman at an electrical equipment company, and would quickly work his way up in the entertainment industry after moving to California with his family a short time later. They were prompted to relocate to the sunny west coast due to their mother's poor health.

Hal got his start in the motion picture business, thanks to his sister Minna who had become a valued assistant to Jack Warner and was even tasked with casting films at Warner Bros. She helped her younger brother to get a job managing a local movie theater and later arranged an introduction to Sam Warner, who hired him to work in the publicity department.

While still in his early 20s Hal became publicity director for the studio and went on to be a production manager for Warner-owned First National by the end of the decade. After his brief demotion to producer, when the two studios merged, Hal was chosen to fill the position of Executive-in-Charge-of-Production for the combined studios, vacated by Darryl Zanuck, who had left to head what would become Twentieth Century Fox.

During his climb to the top, he married popular silent screen comedienne Louise Fazenda in 1927 and the couple had a son together, Brent Wallis.

Like many great producers, Hal Wallis was a visionary. He had good instincts and a gift for seeing possibilities in unique material and artists. His track record for discovering and cultivating screen personalities was an impressive one, making stars out of Bette Davis, Edward G. Robinson, Errol Flynn, Dean Martin & Jerry Lewis, Humphrey Bogart, Shirley MacLaine, Burt Lancaster, Kirk Douglas; and launching Elvis' feature film career.

Hal was one of the few people who could envision the potential in the little known stage play, *Everybody Comes to Rick's*, destined to become the classic big screen feature, *Casablanca*. He believed in the project and was determined to make it into the best motion picture it could be.

Although he tended to be a shy and reserved man who did not appear to actively seek out the spotlight for himself, like some big name producers, getting credit for his accomplishments was important to him. So, when Jack Warner took away his moment of glory by charging up to the stage to accept Hal's Best Picture Oscar for *Casablanca* in 1943, it struck a fatal blow to their business association, which was already in trouble. By this time, Hal had stepped down as head of production, a job which had left him exhausted and robbed him of a home life, and had gone back to being a producer. But Jack Warner reneged on their deal to let him have first pick of any material acquired, and he interfered with Hal's productions.

Intent on having control over the pictures he made, Hal left Warner Bros. in the mid-1940s and became a very successful independent producer, forming his own company which partnered for many years with Paramount and later Universal.

He was never one to turn up his nose at the chance to produce the kind of simple, lighthearted films that could be lucrative at the box office, like his series of screwball Martin & Lewis comedies and the cheesy string of movies he made with Elvis in the 1960s. However, this tough, shrewd businessman was also an artist at heart with a passion for meaningful, emotionally compelling films, such as: *Come Back, Little Sheba*; *King's Row*; *The Rose Tattoo*; and *The Rainmaker*.

Beginning in the 1930s, he enthusiastically made important biopics like *The Life of Emile Zola* and *Juarez*. His love of history and desire to tell the stories of impactful historical figures persisted. Inspiring films about real people and their achievements are scattered throughout his body of work. By the time Hal Wallis decided to bring Maxwell Anderson's *Anne of the Thousand Days* to the big screen, he himself had made monumental contributions to the history of his own industry and was something of a show business legend.

The original Broadway production of *Anne of the Thousand Days* made a strong impression on Hal. He found the theme to be powerful and recognized its screen potential. When he was producing *Becket*, many years later, he and Richard Burton began to discuss the possibility of doing the film version. According to Hal, Richard was a fan of the play and eager to work with the producer again, urged him to buy *Anne of the Thousand Days* and star him in the screen adaptation. If this is true it is more than a little ironic considering how opposed Richard was to doing the film just a few years later.

Hal was surprised to learn that the head of Paramount, Charles Bluhdorn, did not want to follow the success of *Becket* with another historical epic starring Richard Burton. He was furious at Richard because of something that had happened when Richard was asked to do a voice-over and introduction on one of Bluhdorn's films. Initially, the actor had agreed to do it for little money, but when the time came for him to provide the narration, Richard added the stipulation that he would only record the material if Bluhdorn bought Elizabeth Taylor a pair if diamond-and-emerald earrings she liked. Bluhdorn was so angry, he would not buy the earrings and adamantly refused to let Richard work at Paramount following the incident. Hal's efforts to charge the executive's mind were futile, so he decided to end his long association with Paramount and take the project to Universal.

Hal had a problem with the script that he had hired Bridget Boland to write for *Anne of the Thousand Days*. He felt it was too weighty and bookish, so he had it rewritten by John Hale but the screenplay still needed work and all of Max Anderson's heirs had to be in agreement before the property could be handed over. The late author's relatives squabbled for months until Hal took it upon himself to improve the screenplay by cutting and transposing scenes until it was satisfactory.

When television director Charles Jarrott met with him at his hotel in London, the producer took an instant liking to him. The intelligent, clearheaded Englishman with his Tudor style beard even struck Hal as someone who seemed like he could be a member of Henry VIII's court. He was impressed by the work Charles had done on TV, with such projects as *The Young Elizabeth* and *Dr. Jekyll and Mr. Hyde*. Despite what little experience he had with feature film, Hal took a chance and hired him to direct *Anne*.

Obviously, it would require someone special to play Anne Boleyn and when it came to casting the role, Hal took his time. Realizing that none of the well known actresses of the day were suitable for the part, he launched a thorough search for just the right woman, someone with the necessary youth and strength. He had already been disappointed many times after meeting with actresses who did not fit the bill, when Genevieve Bujold's agent called to let him know he had the perfect girl to play Anne, but Hal was desperate, so he told him to bring footage of her to his screening room.

When he viewed three hundred feet from Geneviève's most recent film, he was immediately captivated by her. The image she projected was a striking dichotomy. She appeared fragile and petite but underneath there was a steely strength, intensity and passion. Believing that she was just what he was looking for, Hal agreed to hire the virtual unknown without a screen test. When they did finally meet, while she was on a promotional trip in Hollywood for her movie, they liked each other and it was clear to him that his initial impression of her had been correct. He was convinced that Geneviève would be an ideal Anne Boleyn.

In the role of Henry VIII's first queen, Katherine of Aragon, Hal cast the well established dynamic Greek actress, Irene Papas. He selected first rate British character actors for the smaller roles. He had an easy job of casting in England because as he explained in his memoir, the country was full of great performers.

Anxious for the costumes and jewelry worn in the film to appear totally authentic, Hal worked closely with the accomplished costume designer Margaret Furse who replicated the clothing that Henry and Anne wear in the Holbein paintings.

He was forced to compromise when it came to locations. In some cases his plans to shoot at actual locations were thwarted, since they were unable to get the necessary permission to shoot at Hampton Court, the luxurious palace that was residence to Cardinal Wolsey and then to Henry VIII. Filming at Windsor was out because it was found to be too noisy. However, they were fortunate in being able to use Anne's childhood home of Hever Castle. At the time, Hever belonged to Lord Gavin and Lady Irene Astor and their family, who were very cooperative in allowing filming to take place at the castle. Hal and his wife even became friends with them and spent weekends at the estate.

As a producer who typically involved himself in all aspects of his films, most if not all of what we admire about *Anne of the Thousand Days* can be traced back to Hal Wallis. From his efforts to improve the screenplay, to holding out for the perfect actress to play Anne Boleyn, the close attention he paid to ensuring the film had just the right look and much more, he was the single person most responsible for the film's success. He lived up to his own definition of a real producer, someone who wears many hats and develops a production all the way through, according to their concept of how it should turn out.

Following *Anne*, Hal did just two other historical dramas: *Mary, Queen of Scots* (1971), again with Charles Jarrott, and *The Nelson Affair* (1973). His last film was a return to the western genre which he knew so well, with the popular John Wayne film *Rooster Cogburn* (1975), the sequel to *True Grit*.

After his wife Louise died in 1962, Hal fell in love with the much younger actress Martha Hyer, who co-starred in his movie *The Sons of Katie Elder*. The two wed in 1966 and had a happy life together, remaining married until Hal Wallis' death from complications of diabetes in 1986. Today he is remembered as a legendary producer from the Golden Age of filmmaking

From Stage Play to Screenplay

Maxwell Anderson's play was adapted to the big screen by Richard Sokolove with a screenplay by John Hale and Bridget Boland.

Writer/producer Richard Sokolove, born in 1908, did not have a long list of screen credits to his name but the projects he had worked on were varied. He had co-written the 1946 war-time dramedy *The Magnificent Rogue* and then, in the early 1960s, occasionally wrote for television dramas, including Blake Edwards' detective series *Peter Gunn*, and an anthology series based on stories from the *Saturday Evening Post*, which was titled *The Best of the Post*.

In between his credited writing gigs, Sokolove worked as an associate producer on the 1956 June Allyson-Jack Lemmon musical comedy farce *You Can't Run Away from It*. The only professional experience he had with big screen historical drama, was work he did as an associate producer on a Genghis Khan film called *The Conqueror* (1956), starring John Wayne in the title role.

John Hale, born in Woolwich, London in 1926, a playwright who gained considerable experience writing for British television, in the years leading up to *Anne of the Thousand Days*, beginning in the mid-1960s, with series like the *ITV Play of the Week* and the *ITV Playhouse*. Several of the episodes he wrote for these series were adaptations of D.H. Lawrence stories.

Hale also wrote the 1967 BBC series *The Queen's Traitor*, about a conspiracy to remove Queen Elizabeth I from the throne. The next few years would see Hale working on multiple historical dramas, focusing on the Tudor dynasty, for both the big and small screen.

Although he got a late start in his screenwriting career, Hale quickly found success, and became a prominent novelist as well, penning the espionage thriller *The Whistle Blower*, which was made into the 1986 film starring Michael Caine. In addition to writing, Hale occasionally acted on screen and served as a director at the Old Vic School.

Bridget Boland was the most accomplished screenwriter to work on *Anne of the Thousand Days*. Born in St. George's Hanover Square, London, in 1913, and educated at Oxford, Boland was the daughter of Irish politician John Boland and his wife Eileen. She wrote or co-wrote a number of films including: *Gaslight* (1940); *The Prisoner*; and *War and Peace*. She was also a noted playwright and a novelist.

Even though the stage play for *Anne* had been written by Max Anderson, a woman's perspective, such as Boland's was undoubtedly beneficial to the screenplay, considering it was primarily Anne's story. However, she was, by no means, a stereotypically female author. She was ahead of her time in proving that she could write about traditionally male topics like political intrigue, historical events, and war, which she did numerous times over the years.

Boland felt that she differed from the majority of female authors, in that they tended to succeed at writing domestically set, character-driven stories, while she was disinterested in writing about domestic life and instead thrived on writing heavy drama.

In a sense, *Anne of the Thousand Days* is something of a domestic tale, but definitely not typical of the genre; and so much of the story centers on politics and serious drama that it was well suited to Boland's ability. It also seems appropriate that the ambitious and independently minded Anne Boleyn, who did not conform to the submissive feminine ideal of her time, should have an unconventional authoress like Boland helping to tell her story.

The screenplay provoked mixed reactions. Richard Burton was very critical of the dialogue, but the Academy of Motion Picture Arts and Sciences was impressed enough with the screenplay to nominate it for an Oscar.

Whatever the un-produced script may have looked like on paper, it worked splendidly within the framework of a romantic, costume epic. A film set in the 16th century British royal court could easily come off as dry and stuffy but the high drama of this screenplay, some of which is carried over from the stage play, provides flashes of excitement that holds the audience's interest throughout. It also makes the story accessible to a wide demographic.

In adapting the property for the big screen, some significant changes were made and possibly the most important was shifting the main focus of the story from Henry to Anne. This is even reflected in the ending of the film, after Anne is dead. Unlike the play that gives Henry the last word, in the final scene of the film, little Elizabeth is walking along a path in the gardens of Penshurst Castle and we hear a voice-over, a snippet of Anne's speech from the Tower, in which she predicts that Elizabeth will be a great queen one day.

Anne of the Thousand Days is very much a character drama, offering plenty of juicy material for actors to sink their teeth into, and this is due in large part to the screenplay. The colorful dialogue, verging on campy at times, and the provocatively drawn but refreshingly human characters help to create an opportunity for both Richard Burton and Geneviève Bujold to develop memorable characterizations. As a result, the film stands out, most of all for its performances.

Richard Burton as Henry VIII

Richard Walter Jenkins was born on November 10, 1925 in the South Wales mining town of Pontrhydyfen. He was the 12th of 13 children born to Richard "Dic" Jenkins, and his wife, the former Edith Thomas. His father was an earthy coal miner, known for being a heavy drinker, not unlike many of his peers, but also for his love of poetry and language. His mother was a strong, religious woman who worked hard to take care of her large brood, earning money to feed her children by making sweets and taking in laundry.

Young Richard, usually called "Rich", was only two years old when his mother died, soon after giving birth to his brother Graham. Rich was entrusted to the care of his sister Cecilia "Cis", just 21 at the time, and her newly wed husband Elfred who lived in the nearby town of Port Talbot; while Graham was sent to live with their brother Tom and his wife.

During an interview with Dick Cavett in 1980, Richard said that, although he'd apparently been very attached to his real mother, as a small child, he had no memory of her later on. He seemed to accept Cis, who would go on to have two daughters of her own, as his new mother.

Cis and Rich truly adored each other. According to the 2010 book *Furious Love: Elizabeth Taylor, Richard Burton and the Marriage of the Century*, Richard's autobiographical short story from 1965 titled *A Christmas Story* draws obvious comparisons between his sweet and strikingly pretty, raven-haired sister and his second wife Elizabeth Taylor. However, his relationship with Elfred, who resented how much Cis doted on her bright and already charming kid brother, could be very tense.

He had a generally happy childhood, well-liked and often indulged by his many relatives. As a young boy he seemed more interested in sports than in the performing arts but did pay close attention to the theatrical church sermons he attended, critiquing the ministers in his diary, sometimes even playfully imitating them for his family in mock sermons; and for a time gave his younger brother Graham the impression he might actually go into the clergy. Interestingly, he would memorably play men of the cloth several times during his career, the most famous being the defrocked clergyman Rev. Dr. T Lawrence Shannon in *Night of the Iguana.*

A lifelong book lover, he also wrote and would, years later, elaborate on several pieces from his journal and have them published in magazines. He seemed to have been a hardworking and industrious boy, taking on an assortment of odd jobs to earn money during the Depression era.

By Richard's mid-teens, Elfred was insisting that he get a real job instead of continuing his education, and so he began work as a clerk in a haberdashery, but hated the experience.

Within a couple of years, one of his former teachers who had recognized among other gifts, a potential in Rich for the theater, helped him return to school. Another teacher, Philip Burton, who was involved in local stage and radio productions, would become his mentor.

Philip Burton would eventually become his guardian, and have an inestimable effect on his protégé. He would extensively tutor Rich in Shakespeare, give him vocal training and improve his English, a language which the Welsh-speaking boy had not learned until the age of six but that he grew to love.

At the age of 17, he moved into Philip's lodging house, something that concerned Rich's family, given their suspicions about the middle-aged bachelor's sexuality, but they were reassured by the reputation of the lodging house, which was inhabited by a widow and her two daughters.

Philip Burton was, indeed, a homosexual and it has been suggested that the older man was in love with his adolescent student. Although Rich would eventually experiment with homosexuality, it is believed that this particular relationship was platonic.

Philip's help in preparing him for the theater offered Rich a ticket out of the coal mines, which likely would've been his fate otherwise, like his father and older brothers, instead of being propelled toward his destiny as one of the century's greatest stage and screen actors.

The newly named Richard Burton gained a scholarship to Exeter College at Oxford. Six months later he joined the British air force, serving as an officer in the RAF during the end of World War II.

Richard had already experienced success in the theater before attending Oxford, when he appeared in Emlyn Williams' *The Druid's Rest*. Richard would later claim that it was a good review he received while the play was in London that changed the course of his life, setting him on a definite path to become a professional actor.

He would quickly make a name for himself with memorable performances in plays like *The Lady's Not for Burning* and *The Boy with the Cart*. Around this same time, he launched his film career with a role in the 1949 drama *The Last Days of Dolwyn*, meeting his future wife, 19-year-old Welsh actress Sybil Williams, on the set.

As a captivating stage actor, he would achieve widespread acclaim and was, at one point, seen as the next Laurence Olivier. In his prime, Richard would become that rare combination of a brilliant stage actor and an iconic film star. However, he was often criticized after moving to California and signing a contract with Fox, for neglecting the theater to focus more on films, which included classics like the 1952 gothic romance *My Cousin Rachel* opposite Olivia de Havilland, and Biblical epic *The Robe* in 1953.

He managed to sustain his popularity on stage, particularly when playing King Arthur in the 1960 Broadway musical *Camelot*, reprising the role 20 years later for the revival. His Hamlet in the 1964 production, staged by John Gielgud, is among Broadway history's most legendary performances.

As renowned as Richard Burton became over the years, it is believed by some that he did not reach his full potential of greatness as an actor due to his notoriously heavy drinking, which would plague him for most of his life. It was actually Elizabeth Taylor, perceived much more as a movie star than a serious actress at the time, who was largely responsible for helping Richard to establish himself as a great artist of the cinema, as well as the stage. It was she who encouraged, even insisted that he accept parts in prestige projects that would showcase his talent like *Hamlet* on Broadway, and the films *Night of the Iguana* and *Becket*.

By the time Richard replaced actor Stephen Boyd as Marc Antony in the troubled and excessively over budget 1963 epic *Cleopatra*, he and his spirited but typically level-headed wife Sybil had been married for more than a decade and were the parents of two daughters: Katherine "Kate", born in 1957 and Jessica in 1959. But their lives were soon turned upside down by his scandalous affair with married co-star Elizabeth Taylor, which rocked the world and virtually gave birth to the paparazzi.

Richard, whose combination of animal magnetism and poetic charm made him irresistible to multitudes of women, admitted that affairs were nothing new for him. Sybil had come to accept his rampant infidelity, trusting that he would always return to her. But the scorching relationship he had with Elizabeth would rival the passion of Antony and Cleopatra themselves.

Richard and Elizabeth were very much alike: big, charismatic personalities. They were both intense, complex and shared a strong penchant for alcohol. She was used to getting her own way but preferred strong men like Richard, who wouldn't hesitate to stand up to her.

Their stormy and very public life together was like a big-screen romantic epic. He was also the only one of her seven husbands who was on the same level of celebrity as she was. During the course of their relationship his salary would surpass hers. So, he wasn't stuck in her shadow, and labeled Mr. Elizabeth Taylor like his predecessors.

At first "Liz and Dick" may have just seemed like two flashy, outrageous movie stars flitting around the world from one decadent adventure to another, but their relationship soon elevated the artistic stature of them both. Richard had opportunities to demonstrate his prowess as an actor on a grand scale, while for her, being the wife and frequent co-star of this acclaimed actor with his impressive background in the theater, caused the public to take Elizabeth more seriously as an actress.

One would think that when Richard's success finally eclipsed Elizabeth's in the late 1960s, she would have felt resentful, but although she had been a star for most of her life, this new dynamic suited Elizabeth surprisingly well. She was more than willing to let his career take precedence over hers. She had been uncomfortable during marriages in which she was the primary breadwinner.

Elizabeth had three children from previous unions plus a daughter, Maria, whom she had adopted with Richard, and had, many years before, expressed the opinion that it was more important to focus on being a mother than an actress. More recently she had made it clear she was happy to be "Mrs. Burton".

Considering Elizabeth's persona as a fickle, home-wrecking siren and Burton's reputation as a serial philanderer, the threat of infidelity would have seemed a valid concern to anyone romantically involved with either of them. Richard and Elizabeth fought as passionately as they loved, with rows comparable to scenes from their 1966 film *Who's Afraid of Virginia Woolf?*

By the time *Anne of the Thousand Days* began production in the spring of 1969, it had been over seven years since the onset of the drama-fueled love affair that led to their marriage in 1964. The pair had remained so madly, obsessively and tenderly in love with one another, it was hard to imagine, despite the long lists of previous relationships each had enjoyed, that anyone could ever come between them. And yet, jealousy was mutual for this ultra-glamorous power couple.

Elizabeth had a history of behaving as if she was seriously threatened by Richard's leading ladies. When he co-starred with his old flame, Claire Bloom, in 1965's *The Spy Who Came in from the Cold*, her discomfort was very apparent to Bloom, herself, who later wrote about it in her 1995 memoir. But Elizabeth would appear to feel even more threatened by Richard's *Anne of the Thousand Days* love interest, the lovely, young, effervescent Geneviève Bujold.

A few months before taking on the role of Henry VIII, he bought a pear shaped pearl called La Peregrina, for Elizabeth, which had once belonged to Henry VIII's daughter Queen Mary I. It was set into a ruby and diamond necklace. Richard paid $37,000. However, this extravagant bauble didn't even come close to the most expensive piece of jewelry he bought for her, that would be the famous 69.42 karat diamond which cost Richard $1.1 million in 1969 and subsequently became known as the Taylor-Burton diamond, which would also be made into a necklace.

The Burtons sailed to London on their yacht Kalizma in May of 1969 to begin filming of *Anne of the Thousand Days*. When they arrived, docking the vessel, just outside the House of Parliament, it created quite a frenzy among the secretaries who stood at the windows gaping at them.

Richard had grudgingly prepared for the project over the past few weeks, doing research and growing a beard, while he and Elizabeth were vacationing in their beloved Puerto Vallarta with their children. But he felt such little motivation, Elizabeth had to make him learn his lines. Richard had remained unenthusiastic about his role, feeling that Henry VIII was not a challenging character for an actor. He was also very critical of the script's dialogue, judging it to be lacking in subtlety and of poor quality. But as someone who loved poetry and treasured great literature he undoubtedly had high standards.

During his two hour-long drives from the studio back to the Kalizma each day, he would try to figure out ways to make the part a more interesting one to play. He settled on the idea of making the king a charming but demonic man, who could quickly fly into a rage.

Henry was known for having a terrible temper, a trait he had in common with Richard, who was no stranger to fury. The cynicism and extreme intelligence that he brought to the role were also qualities that Richard, himself, clearly possessed. And whether intentional or not, he made Henry sexy, or at least sexier than the image audiences previously had of this notorious monarch.

One thing that Richard and Geneviève's performances had in common was that they both portrayed their characters as startlingly frank, a quality that in all likelihood, neither Henry nor Anne would have exhibited very often. They were products of their environment. Diplomacy, subtlety and flattery, were all traits that were ingrained into those bred at the royal courts of Europe in this era. There is evidence that Henry and Anne were prone to use a clever, artful approach in expressing themselves than the earthy, direct tone we see in these interpretations of the characters or the dialogue written for them.

As Richard pointed out while doing press for the film, this version of Henry VIII was fashioned by Maxwell Anderson and others, as opposed to being a true historical representation. Discussing previous interpretations of Henry VIII, Richard praised the power of Charles Laughton's memorable portrayal. But he made it clear that he was not trying to do the character the way Laughton had, or to look the part. Instead, his approach was to play Henry as a sort of extension of himself.

In the film *Anne of the Thousand Days*, Henry was not as tortured as he was in Anderson's original work. The regret-filled closing speech following Anne's death, which could have helped Richard to get the Oscar, was left out of the screen adaptation. This Henry ended up being an interesting mixture between the colorful, greedy narcissist we know so well, and the more human, complex man from the stage play.

The real Henry VIII was attractive, athletic and charming in his youth. It was only during his later years that he turned into the bloated, raging tyrant that would be his legacy. While Richard's performance did give us a fleeting glimpse of the monster Henry would become, it was more of a prototype for modern depictions of Henry, such as Jonathan Rhys Meyers' incarnation for TV series *The Tudors*.

In the context of an interview on the set of *Anne*, Richard claimed that he found Henry fascinating, even comparing him to Hamlet, albeit on a larger scale. He went through a wide variety of adjectives that could be used to describe Henry, from ruthless, to melancholic to brilliant.

How sincere he was in these comments is hard to tell, after all he was promoting the movie, so he had every reason to make Henry sound as exciting as possible. However, it is likely that after finding a way to make the character more stimulating, Richard had come to appreciate Henry more than he did in the early days of production.

Perhaps the most compelling sign that the role was growing on him was when he brought up the fact that the Tudor king was actually Anglo-Welsh, like himself. Knowing how much pride Richard took in being a Welshman, this could be a telling gesture.

Although Elizabeth had been judged too old to play Anne, and only ended up with a cameo in the film, Richard believed she would have been marvelous in the part. It's easy to imagine her as the feisty, strong-willed femme fatale. The chemistry and fire between Richard and Elizabeth that was apparent, both in their personal lives and onscreen, would have worked very well in this movie; but with two such larger than life personalities, the film's dynamic would have been altered significantly.

While the truth about Richard's personal feelings toward the French-Canadian actress Geneviève Bujold, who was ultimately cast as Anne Boleyn, is murky at best, their onscreen chemistry and her interpretation of Anne are nothing short of magical.

Following his acclaimed Academy Award-nominated performance in *Anne of the Thousand Days*, Richard Burton's screen career took a downturn, as he appeared in many forgettable films over the next decade. He would only be nominated for one more Oscar following *Anne of the Thousand Days* and that was for Best Actor in a Leading Role in the 1977 film *Equus*, which he lost.

One of the many honors he did receive was a CBE (Commander of the British Empire) at Buckingham Palace, on his 45th birthday in 1970. He believed the reason he wasn't granted a knighthood was because he had switched his residence from London to the Swiss town of Céligny in order to avoid paying taxes.

Other career highlights in his later years include the 1978 action-adventure movie *Wild Geese*, which was a big hit in Europe, the TV mini-series *Wagner*, co-starring Laurence Olivier, and a highly praised performance as O'Brien in his last film *1984*.

Richard and Elizabeth co-starred in *Divorce His – Divorce Hers*, in 1973, just before their real life divorce. Of course, the couple famously remarried in 1975 only to divorce again less than a year later. They reteamed on the stage for a Broadway revival of *Private Lives* in 1983. He was married to model/actress Suzy Hunt, 1976-1982. Richard's last wife was production assistant Sally Hay from July of 1983 until his death 13 months later.

Although he was on the wagon for much of his marriage to Suzy Hunt, who was credited with keeping him sober, Richard's notorious history of alcohol abuse deeply impacted his health. He died of a cerebral hemorrhage on August 5, 1984 at the age of 58.

Until the very end, it seemed that the two sides of Richard Burton, the scholarly, poetic, brilliant Shakespearian actor and the dazzling, rakish Hollywood playboy would compete for predominance in the public eye. It is actually the combination of all these things that make him so fascinating. At the age of 50, Richard Burton said that the best role he ever played was his own life.

Geneviève Bujold as Anne Boleyn

On the verge of international fame, 27-year-old Geneviève Bujold could not bear to watch herself playing the title role in *Anne of the Thousand Days* at the first press screening in 1969. She'd had some success as an actress in French cinema and in her home country of Canada, but Geneviève was all but unknown in America.

This lavish Hal B. Wallis film, which had her starring as a queen opposite Hollywood royalty, Richard Burton, could very well be her big break. Although Geneviève had yet to see this picture, which could potentially change her life forever, she elected to remain at her hotel during the screening itself, only returning to mingle with the guests in the foyer of the theater afterwards.

In addition to disliking the sound of her own voice, she knew that she would be in no shape to speak to people after the screening, if she had to watch herself acting in a movie which was as performance driven as this one. She finally saw the film at Hal Wallis' home a few nights later. But it wasn't until she viewed *Anne of the Thousand Days* for the second time, when it was screened at a royal command performance, that she was able to relax and enjoy the picture.

While Geneviève has always been forthcoming about her fears and insecurities, she also readily acknowledges her strength, and it must have taken a strong will for the very ambitious young actress to turn down Hal Wallis' request for a screen test, many months earlier, when he was considering her for the part of Anne Boleyn.

As it happened, saying no to Wallis was the best move she could have made, because the sort of spirit she demonstrated in refusing to do the screen test reminded him of Anne, herself, and the role was soon hers.

The performance, which sparked Wallis' interest, was from the Canadian film *Isabel* in which Geneviève plays the title character, a woman who thinks she is going insane because she's starting to see ghosts. *Isabel* was written and directed by her husband at the time, Canadian filmmaker Paul Almond. He had already directed her in several episodes of the TV series *Festival,* as well as the film *Between Sweet and Salt Water* in 1967.

Mostly unknown to American audiences and living in the east end of Montreal at the time, she was extremely surprised to get a call from Hal Wallis, who knew after viewing footage from *Isabel* that he'd found the female lead for his next major motion picture. She knew how important a filmmaker Wallis was and what starring in one of his movies could mean to her future as an actress, but she had no way of knowing that *Anne of the Thousand Days*, and her performance in it, would define her career more than any other project.

Geneviève Bujold was brought up in a world very different from the one in which she now found herself. She was born July 1, 1942, in Montreal, Québec into a devoutly Catholic, working class family, which was mainly of French-Canadian descent with a bit of Irish. Her father, Joseph, worked as a bus driver and her mother, Laurette, was a maid employed at the childhood home of René Lévesque, Québec's premiere 1976-1985.

Geneviève was educated at the very strict Hochelaga Convent, which left a lasting emotional impression on her. This was a bleak time for Geneviève, in which she tried to hold on to the hope that she would find light in the world beyond. In discussing her experience at convent school, in a 1978 *People* magazine interview, she described how she had learned to feel guilty about a lot of things and that although she was not as prone to guilt as she had once been, it could still be a problem.

Considering she would go on to give some of her most memorable performances as rebellious women on screen, it seems fitting that an act of defiance was responsible for her departure from school during her 12th year, when she was expelled after being caught reading a provocative novel that was not from the convent library. She tried another convent school but clashed with one of the nuns.

Reflecting on her family in later years, she expressed admiration for her parents and was clearly influenced, as a young woman, by their conservative lifestyle. Her older sister also made a big impression on Geneviève when she was growing up, particularly because of her exceptional intelligence, which Geneviève could find intimidating.

Like most teenage girls of her generation, one of her favorite pastimes was listening to Elvis Presley records, even though in her case, she couldn't understand the lyrics because she didn't speak English until she was 18 years old.

Also interested in ballet and theater, Geneviève gravitated toward performing at an early age. Following her exit from the convent school, she enrolled at Montreal's Conservatoire d'art dramatique, where she studied classical French dramatic arts.

She earned her tuition for the conservatoire by working as an usherette in a Montreal movie theater. This experience was also beneficial to her in that she had the opportunity to study Hollywood acting. Just before graduation she dropped out of Conservatoire d'art Dramatique to accept a role in a local theater production of *The Barber of Seville*, when she was 19 years old.

Around this time there was also a brief marriage to a biology student, which is rarely mentioned. The union only lasted 18 months, and Geneviève later admitted it was just for the benefit of a lawfully recognized physical relationship.

Once she became a working actress, things happened quickly for Geneviève, who appeared in a number of TV series and movies over the next couple of years. While on tour in France with a Montreal theater company, she accepted a part in the film *La guerre est finie* (*The War is Over*), directed by Alain Resnais, whose mother had recommended her to him.

The political drama, which featured Geneviève opposite Yves Montand, was quickly followed by another French film, Philippe de Broca's wartime farce *King of Hearts*, starring Alan Bates as Charles, a British soldier in World War I, trying to evacuate patients of a mental institution who believe him to be their king. She gives a wonderful performance as Coquelicot, an enchanting and innocent girl who tenderly seduces Charles.

Geneviève was long referred to as a childlike woman and in the role of Coquelicot, she makes the most of her natural wistfulness and vulnerability. It is this same childlike quality, enhanced by her petite stature and impish face, that helped her balance the toughness and iron will that she would soon project in the role of Anne Boleyn.

King of Hearts was not a big hit when it was first released in 1966 but it would go on to become a cult classic, even playing in the same theater in Cambridge, Massachusetts for five years in the 1970s.

Next Geneviève played the love interest in Jean-Paul Belmondo's crime dramedy *The Thief of Paris* from acclaimed filmmaker Louis Malle. One of her most notable projects during this time was the American TV movie *Saint Joan*, in which she played Joan of Arc. The performance earned her critical praise and an Emmy nomination.

Seeing Geneviève's many luminous appearances on-screen, it's obvious the camera loves her, and from the feelings she expressed about screen acting to *Time*, the love is mutual. She doesn't feel fully alive until she's in front of a camera. She emphasizes how completely the camera sees you. For Geneviève the camera offers a mixture of both safety and freedom. She points out that it is impossible to fake your way through things on camera but makes it clear that she herself has no need to fake it.

Geneviève was also enjoying an eventful personal life during this period, having married her live-in boyfriend of two years, Paul Almond, by now and giving birth to their son Matthew in 1968. It wasn't until she had learned that she was pregnant that the couple decided to marry. This was one of the times in her life when Geneviève's traditional upbringing would take precedence over her independence and non-conformist lifestyle.

In this era of the sexual revolution, when well-known actresses were starting to openly bear children out of wedlock., she was anxious to give her child a sense of security and protect him from the ridicule that was still provoked by illegitimacy.

Plus, she wanted to spare her parents any pain, so she chose a more conventional life.

However, the marriage was over by 1973. Geneviève would say that she was the one who ended it, when she fell in love with someone else. She appeared to have a close relationship with Matt, who she raised on her own for several years in Malibu, following the divorce.

She was devastated when Matt decided to move back to Canada to live with his father at the age of nine. But Geneviève got along well enough with her ex-husband to continue to work on projects with him many years after they split up.

Geneviève felt that she was a blank slate, going into *Anne of the Thousand Days*. But it would seem that slate was already inscribed with some of the most indelible qualities attributed to Anne herself, including but not limited to her marked independence and her tendency to be opinionated, two characteristics that she recognized in herself. The latter was obvious to Richard Burton during their very first meeting in Paris, shortly before filming began.

If there was one aspect of *Anne of the Thousand Days* that set it apart from the many other Anne Boleyn biopics and from the average historical costume drama, it was the unforgettable performance of Geneviève Bujold: her feistiness, effervescence, smoldering sensuality and her originality. She brought to life the Anne Boleyn of our imaginations, the woman we believe that she either was or should have been.

Despite the amazing talent that surrounded her in this film, the brilliant veteran actors, especially her iconic male lead, this was first and foremost Geneviève's movie and not just because the story primarily focused on Anne. Inside that particular role in that setting, she was the center of attention, shining more brightly than anyone or anything else.

It's hard to believe the notion that Richard Burton, at the height of his career, might have felt threatened by this young ingénue who was still largely unknown outside of Canada, but considering his intelligence, instincts and alertness to being even slightly upstaged by other actors, he probably noticed her charisma and her ability to sometimes dominate their scenes together.

An indication that her dynamic performance may have brought out some sort of insecurities in Richard is the fact that he was critical of her voice on more than one occasion, commenting in his diary about how much more powerful his voice was and that he could out-project her merely by whispering. This is an area where he must have felt very sure of himself. After all, how many actors could have competed with Richard Burton's deep, resonate, mellifluent voice?

Richard could be privately critical of Geneviève in a number of ways, including his unfavorable comparisons of her to Elizabeth Taylor, who he thought would have been better in the part, feeling that although Geneviève would be adequate, the role called for more fire and brightness than she could bring to it.

But despite the fault he found with her, Geneviève and Richard appeared to get along well most of the time. In an interview with *Box Office Mojo*, she shared fond memories of working with Richard Burton, recalling how he would recite verse when a group of them went to lunch together. She also highly praised him when she accepted her Golden Globe award, for *Anne*.

It is likely that in another movie Richard would have overshadowed Geneviève, but this was her moment. There's a reason why this performance stands out among the dozens of others she's given over the years. This is the role we instantly associate with her, and it isn't just because *Anne of the Thousand Days* is a great film; it's because Geneviève's portrayal of Anne, above all else makes it great.

Geneviève takes her preparation as an actress very seriously. She also feels it is important to remain open in her work. After she has read a script that stays with her, she feeds all her observations from her daily life into the role she is preparing to play. In the interview with *Box Office Mojo*, Geneviève talked about all the help she had in preparing for *Anne of the Thousand Days*, which included an acting coach.

Geneviève loved and admired the character she was playing. She did a lot of research on Anne Boleyn, and said in an interview during filming, that she wished she could have met her. She said that she felt like she did know Anne, which is easy to believe, watching her play the part. Geneviève's performance demonstrates a deep understanding of the character.

Anne Boleyn's story has been dramatized many times, but no one has played Anne more compellingly on screen than Geneviève Bujold. She makes us root for Anne despite the fallen queen's much maligned reputation. But her interpretation of Anne is a complex one. Instead of the king's coquettish, opportunistic whore, or as one of Henry's lawfully wedded victims, she is a multi-dimensional human being, who at one moment, can be as formidable as Henry himself and the next as vulnerable as a child.

Hal Wallis wanted to immediately cast Geneviève as another historical figure who famously met her end on the scaffold, Mary Stuart, in the film *Mary, Queen of Scots* (1971). But having just come off playing a queen, she was not ready to take her place on the throne again so soon, and was also concerned about being typecast.

Geneviève instead chose to reteam with Irene Papas in another historical drama 1971's *Trojan Women*.

Vanessa Redgrave would go on to play the title role in *Mary, Queen of Scots*, opposite Glenda Jackson, who was cast as Elizabeth I. Charles Jarrott directed the picture, which has been referred to as a sequel to *Anne of the Thousand Days*. Geneviève's refusal to star in the movie resulted in a lawsuit with Universal. However, she has a long history of choosing roles for artistic reasons rather than commercial potential and she is content to live simply.

In order to fulfill her contract with Universal she would eventually co-star in the 1974 disaster epic *Earthquake*. Other career highlights include: the 1978 hospital mystery *Coma*, costarring Michael Douglas, the Sherlock Holmes film *Murder By Decree* (1979) with Christopher Plummer, and the 1988 thriller *Dead Ringers*, opposite Jeremy Irons.

In 1980, at the age of 37, she gave birth to her son Emmanuel Claude Bujold, whose father is carpenter Dennis Hastings, Geneviève's partner since 1977. The couple first met when Hastings was building her home.

On June 1, 2018 Geneviève received the Governor General's Performing Arts Award, which is the most prestigious honor that can be bestowed on a performing artist in Canada. She still works, when the right project comes along, applying the same dedication and thoughtfulness to her roles as always. In recent years she costarred with Bruce Dern in the drama *Northern Borders* (2013) and in the award-winning *Chorus* (2015).

It would seem that Geneviève Bujold and Anne Boleyn owe much to one another. Because of her role as Anne, Geneviève was launched into Hollywood stardom. Overnight a new world was opened up to the little-known French-Canadian actress. Fifty years later, the character is still her best remembered by American audiences.

As a historical figure, Anne Boleyn has benefited greatly from Geneviève's performance because it helped to humanize her, following centuries of Anne mainly being a symbol of various things: anti-Protestant propaganda, scheming women, vixens, ambition, a casualty of Henry VIII's tyranny.

Geneviève made us see Anne as someone we could care about, even relate to on a certain level. She turned traits previously viewed as flaws into qualities worthy of admiration. Her Anne was strong, determined, smart, brave and self-assured.

An Impressive Cast of Supporting Players

Anne of the Thousand Days had an exceptional supporting cast. These were very talented and charismatic actors who were capable of holding an audience's attention instead of fading into the background when playing a scene with one of the stars. This was more than just the actors' tricks that Richard Burton alluded to when describing the challenges he faced trying to avoid being upstaged by his castmates.

The supporting roles were all well cast in *Anne of the Thousand Days*, from key players down to the bit parts, but it was Anthony Quayle who made an indelible mark on the film, as the shrewd, calculating Cardinal Thomas Wolsey, Archbishop of York and Lord Chancellor of England. Wolsey is the long-time trusted advisor to Henry, and the most important man in England after the king himself, but his power is eventually usurped by Anne Boleyn, who considers him an enemy. Although Wolsey is not intended to be likable, Quayle, who plays the character flawlessly, is able to elicit sympathy for him when necessary and humanize Wolsey, the way Geneviève Bujold does for Anne.

John Anthony Quayle was born September 7, 1913 in Ainsdale, England. Although his father, a Lancashire lawyer, was a devotee of the theater who would take his family to see all the touring companies that came to town, Anthony was expected to have a career in the family drug business. However, his lack of aptitude for physics or chemistry made it clear to Anthony that this was not his field; and he decided he could only be successful in either writing or acting.

It was in Vaudeville that Anthony made his stage debut in 1931, but he quickly graduated to proper theater, joining the Old Vic Theatre in 1932, where he transitioned into a fine Shakespearian actor. While touring with the Old Vic he played Laertes in *Hamlet* and starred in the title role of *Henry V*. His first New York play was in *The Country Wife* in 1936. Soon after serving as a major of artillery in WWII, he was back on stage in *The Rivals*.

Anthony expanded his career around this time, helming *Crime and Punishment* before distinguishing himself as director of The Shakespeare Memorial Theatre at Stratford Upon-Avon in 1948. He had great success managing the theater and stayed in the position until 1956.

Although Anthony dabbled in films early on, he did not truly establish an onscreen career until the 1950s, when he appeared in movies like Hitchcock's *The Wrong Man* (1956) and the 1957 romance drama *Woman in a Dressing Gown*. At the same time, he frequently worked on TV.

His most notable film prior to *Anne of the Thousand Days* was *Lawrence of Arabia* (1960), in which he played Colonel Brighton. While he was noted for his versatility and acted in a wide range of films from romance to suspense thrillers to action flicks like *Tarzan's Greatest Adventure*, Anthony made a number of prominent historical dramas in the 1960s for which he was well suited, due in part, to his classical training.

Anthony married stage actress Hermione Hannen in 1934. The couple divorced in 1941. He was married to second wife, Dorothy Hyson, from 1947 until his death in 1989. With Hyson he had three children including actress Jenny Quayle.

In his Oscar-nominated depiction of Wolsey, Anthony projected a mixture of authoritarian, diplomat and wily politician who understood Henry VIII perhaps better than Henry understood himself. He was convincing as a man who, in some ways, seemed like a father figure to Henry and could easily take over when the impetuous king was too distracted by other matters to lead the country.

Anthony cleverly managed to play the powerful and ambitious cardinal with dignity but very little, if any, pretension, leaving the pomposity and arrogance to Henry. At moments he almost seems an everyman, who still retains remnants of his humble background as a butcher's son. Whether Anthony did this intentionally or not, it was helpful in fleshing out the character.

Instead of falling back on the image of a pious, self-important church leader and statesman, Anthony gives Wolsey dimension and makes him more interesting by giving us a glimpse of the man who's had to struggle to achieve his status.

Anthony stayed busy over the next 20 years, especially on television, doing many TV movies and series including *The Six Wives of Henry VIII* in 1970, which he narrated. He frequently acted in Biblical projects like *Moses The Lawgiver* (1974), and as well as other historical dramas like *The Last Days of Pompeii* (1984). He served as director of the touring company Compass, which he had founded in 1984, and was knighted in 1985. Anthony continued to work until shortly before his death from cancer in 1989 at the age of 76.

≈≈≈≈≈

The lawyer and statesman Thomas Cromwell, first Earl of Essex, has not always been depicted as a straightforward villain but in *Anne of the Thousand Days* that's really the only way he is presented to us. His ambition and ruthless plotting make formidable power seekers, like Cardinal Wolsey and Anne Boleyn, look like lambs by comparison.

Cromwell, who was chief minister to Henry VIII from 1532 to 1540, is characterized as a man of little or no conscience who would use any means necessary to accomplish his objectives, including, as shown in one memorable scene, torture. Even Henry, far from a paragon of virtue himself, seems disgusted by Cromwell, merely tolerating him as a necessary evil, someone to device schemes and carry out the king's dirty work. John Colicos was able to embody this version of Cromwell to a very impressive extent.

The fact that he was so convincing in the part is due mainly to his talent as an actor but John's physical appearance was a real advantage as well. There was something sinister in his face, particularly his dark piercing eyes and sly smile, which could come across as serpentine in his more menacing roles, such as this.

John Colicos was born in Toronto, Ontario, Canada on December 10, 1928 to a Canadian mother and a Greek father. He grew up in Montreal. His first acting role was Jesus Christ in a Biblical pageant, ironic considering all the wicked characters that would later be his mainstay.

Like Richard Burton and Anthony Quayle, John built a reputation in the theater early on, as a gifted Shakespearian actor. One highlight of his career was when, at the age of 22, he played the title role in *King Lear* at the Old Vic in London, making him the youngest actor to ever play the part. In 1957 he would play the role of Edmund in *King Lear* when he made his New York theater debut. But his association with the play didn't end there. He would again take on the role of the emotionally disturbed king in 1964 at Canada's Stratford Festival.

He was cast in a variety of roles at the American Shakespeare Festival Theatre including his much admired Petruchio in *The Taming of the Shrew*. The year before starting work on *Anne of the Thousand Days*, John gave one of his most acclaimed performances, playing Winston Churchill in the controversial play *Soldiers* on the London stage in 1968. He was also a prolific television actor throughout his career. In the 50s and 60s he appeared in a number of crime shows like *The Defenders* and action series, such as *Mission Impossible*.

Like many of his castmates on *Anne of the Thousand Days*, John took his craft seriously. He even had a 4,000 volume theatrical research library in his home.

John married Mona McHenry in 1956. The couple, who had two sons together, divorced in 1981. Their son Nicholas Colicos is also an actor.

He didn't mind portraying villains. He found villains more interesting and more fun than heroes. His interpretation of Thomas Cromwell may have been one of his most interesting villains and is likely his best remembered feature film performance.

His greatest success came late in life with sci-fi projects like the film and TV series *Battlestar Galactica* in the late 1970s and *Star Trek*: *Deep Space Nine* (1994-1998), which was one of his last jobs before his death in 2000 at the age of 71, following multiple heart attacks.

≈≈≈≈≈

The highly revered Michael Hordern who played Anne's father, Thomas Boleyn, was a very down to earth man who didn't become a professional actor until his late 20s. Born on October 3, 1911 in Berkhamsted, Hertfordshire, England, he had briefly worked as an educator and as a salesman before he took on the role of Lodovico in a 1937 stage production of *Othello*. His conventional, real world experience was probably one of the things that helped to keep him grounded after his theatrical career took off.

Michael's preference for simple country living and his love of fishing was not only in sharp contrast to so many of his fast-living show business peers but also to Thomas Boleyn, who is usually depicted as a social climbing mercenary, materialistic courtier, actively pimping out his daughters in exchange for the King's favor. Michael portrays him as more of a practical, realistic but not completely unsympathetic father, so eager to maintain if not improve his standard of living, he allows Mary and Anne to be used by Henry.

Of course, this departure to our traditional concept of Thomas Boleyn is not entirely due to Michael's approach to the character. The script is partially responsible. However, Michael was known not only for being extremely talented but for being very original.

His first appearance onscreen was in the 1939 dramedy *A Girl Must Live*. He had a couple of uncredited movie roles soon after, but his career was put on hold for several years with the outbreak of World War II, during which he served as a lieutenant commander in the Navy.

He married actress Eveline Mortimer in 1943. The couple had one daughter together.

Michael's career in the theater finally took off with the hit play *Dear Murderer*, and while playing Mr. Toad of *Toad of Toad Hall* at Stratford-Upon-Avon for Christmas of 1948 and 1949. Over the next few years he delivered impressive performances in several plays including the demanding title role in Chekhov's *Ivanhoe* and played Polonius to a young Richard Burton's Hamlet during the Old Vic's 1953-1954 season. However, Michael did not make his Broadway debut until 1959, when he co-starred in *Moonbirds*.

He did many films and TV projects from the late 1940s onward, mainly playing character roles, being especially adept at such roles, due in part, to his amazing range. He was occasionally cast in some interesting leads, portraying Maxim De Winter in a 1947 TV movie adaptation of *Rebecca*.

By the time *Anne of the Thousand Days* began production, Michael had already worked with Richard Burton, who was enormously impressed by the actor, several times including: *Cleopatra*; *The V.I.P.s* (1963); *The Spy Who Came in from the Cold* (1965); and *The Taming of the Shrew* (1967).

Michael Hordern added to the high quality of the production. Often cast as straight-laced authority figures or as aristocrats, he was a good fit for the role of Thomas Boleyn. He also helped to soften his character's edges with a hint of his own natural warmth and perhaps because as a great comedic actor he always tried to find humor in the roles he played.

Michael was a prolific actor for the rest of his career acting in dozens of projects for both the big and small screen, after *Anne of the Thousand Days*. His body of work was a strikingly eclectic mixture ranging from voicing Badger in the animated 1980s series *Wind in the Willows* to co-starring in several TV adaptations of Shakespearian plays. He also did some high profile features in his later years including *Gandhi* in which he played Sir George Hodge.

Michael Hordern was knighted in 1985 and died 10 years later of kidney disease at the age of 83.

≈ ≈ ≈ ≈ ≈

Irene Papas did not portray Henry's first wife, Katherine of Aragon, as the helpless victim that many assume she was but rather as a fighter. It was the type of role Irene said she liked to play, describing herself as a fighter. While the deep piety that Queen Katherine was known for, is clearly present in the performance, alongside it is passion and even ferocity at moments, as she struggles to hold onto her place as Queen Consort of England and to her daughter Mary's claim to the throne. As we know, Katherine did not win but she did not go quietly.

Irene Papas was born Eirini Lelékou September 3, 1926 in Chiliomodi, Corinth, Greece. Prior to *Anne of the Thousand Days* she was best known to American audiences for the 1961 action-adventure drama *The Guns of Navarone*, in which she worked with Anthony Quayle, and for the iconic 1964 dramedy *Zorba the Greek*. She also did several television shows over the years, including the 1968 mini-series *Odissea*, based on Homer's *The Iliad* and *The Odyssey*.

Irene was a popular choice for the lead in feature film adaptations of classical Greek dramas, playing the title roles in *Electra* and in *Antigone* during the early 1960s. Irene's powerful presence and gravitas made her a natural for iconic heroines from historical drama, and it was these very traits that set her apart from the frothy Hollywood starlets of the era. It was not Irene's goal to portray glamorous sirens. With an attitude that was progressive for her time, she preferred playing strong independent women.

Although she had no trouble with prominent roles, Irene played a lot of bit parts as well, explaining to Roger Ebert, when he interviewed her during the filming of *Anne of the Thousand Days*, that she didn't have too much pride to turn down such roles, and the money was good.

Despite her unconventional good looks, thick accent and the limited number of leading men tall enough to star opposite the 5'10 actress, during this era when the male lead *had* to be taller than his love interest, Irene still managed to make her mark in the international cinema and greatly impressed such legends as Federico Fellini and her friend/co-star Katharine Hepburn.

She married the director/writer/actor Alkis Papas in 1943 but the couple divorced four years later. She did, however, star in his 1959 romantic comedy *Psit…koritsia!* She married producer José Kohn in 1957 but the union was later annulled.

In addition to acting, Irene was a singer who recorded and contributed to several albums over the years, including the jazz record *Songs of Theodorakis*, which came out the year before *Anne of the Thousand Days*. She was also a published poet, but mainly wrote poetry for herself, apparently as a sort of catharsis when she going through hard times.

Irene gives a very compelling performance in *Anne* and keeps her dignity through it all, even while begging Henry not to have their marriage annulled. With a lesser actress, the character would have come across as pitiful but Irene projected strength, confidence and nobility. At times our sympathies are torn between Katherine and the film's heroine, Anne Boleyn.

Irene worked steadily until 2003, doing both classical and contemporary projects. One of her last roles was Drosoula in the 2001 big screen romantic drama *Captain Corelli's Mandolin* starring Nicolas Cage and Penélope Cruz.

Since her retirement from acting, she has opened an alternative drama school in Greece, the Irene Papas – Athens School. In 2017 it was announced that the National Theater of Greece would relocate their drama school to the venue.

≈≈≈≈≈

Anne of the Thousand Days featured a mix of acclaimed, long established actors and exciting newcomers. The film would be young Terence Wilton's big screen debut. Terence played Anne Boleyn's fiancé Lord Percy. Originally from Brighton, England, he had little experience going into *Anne*. He had started doing television a few years earlier, beginning with an episode of *Liars* in 1966. This was followed by small roles in the 1967 mini-series *Vanity Fair*, and TV movie *The Bastard King*. Just before *Anne*, he did an episode of *Rouges' Gallery*.

Terence, who has since acquired a reputation as a very talented stage actor, appeared the antithesis to Henry VIII. In his portrayal of Percy, the fresh-faced, actor, with his gentle demeanor and projection of sincerity, almost couldn't have been more opposite from the loud, overbearing, cynical Henry.

The fact that the two rivals are so different underscore Anne's deep resentment and bitterness when she is forced to give up Percy so that Henry can have her. Although Anne does grow to love Henry eventually, it is important at the beginning of the film to make it seem nearly impossible for a woman in love with a man like Percy to be attracted to Henry.

Terence was ideal as Lord Percy, and the performance paid off for him as well, providing his first real break in show business. Following *Anne*, Terence did a number of TV projects including a production of *Hamlet* in 1971 and several episodes of *Doctor Who*. He has worked extensively as a Shakespearian actor and has taught drama at Blackheath High School for Girls alongside his wife actress Lucy Tregear and their daughter.

≈≈≈≈≈

In the role of Anne Boleyn's mother, Elizabeth Boleyn, was actress Katharine Blake, who was married to the film's director Charles Jarrott at the time. People would assume that Elizabeth would be a sexy and charming woman, considering she was mother to two of Henry VIII's favorite mistresses, and Katharine brought just the right amount of spirit and a hint of mysterious sex appeal to the role. Her face, which faintly resembled both Geneviève Bujold and Valerie

Gearon, who played Mary Boleyn, had an aristocratic look but it would light up with her flirtatious smile and the twinkle in her eye.

Katharine Blake was born Illonne Katharine Inglestone in Johannesburg, South Africa on September 11, 1921. Her first appearance on screen was as Catherine Earnshaw in a television production of *Wuthering Heights* in 1948. She continued to work mainly on TV over the next two decades, acting in dozens of series such as the *ITV Play of the Week*; *Folio*; and *The Avengers*. Katharine did many dramas and mystery series but also quite a bit of historical drama, including an episode of *Thursday Theatre* in 1964, titled *The Young Elizabeth* in which she played Mary Boleyn, just five years before playing Mary's mother in *Anne of the Thousand Days*.

Katharine Blake was also a television writer, penning a 1966 episode of BBC drama *The Wednesday Play* and an episode of the supernatural themed miniseries *Haunted* (1967).

Before her marriage to Charles Jarrott (1959-1982), Katharine was married to actor/filmmaker David Greene (1948-1959) and to actor Anthony Jacobs (1942-1948). She had one daughter with each of her first two husbands.

Like many of the other supporting actors on *Anne of the Thousand Days*, Katharine made the most of her limited screen time. Without overshadowing the principal players, she managed to make a real impression as a skillful courtier who could also be a loving mother and, at the same time, sultry enough to make us wonder if there could be some truth in Henry's joke about an affair between the two of them.

Katharine continued to act until 1981, appearing in many television dramas over the years including the acclaimed Henry Tudor series *The Shadow of the Tower* and the anthology program *Armchair Theatre*. She died in 1991 at the age of 69.

≈≈≈≈≈

While other films have explored Mary Boleyn's romance with Henry VIII, in this movie we are introduced to Mary after she has been impregnated and discarded by Henry, who has already moved on to her sister Anne. Valerie Gearon is convincing as the bitter, heartbroken and naturally resentful Mary, warning Anne not to make the same mistake.

Valerie Gearon was born in Newport, Monmouthshire, Wales in 1937. She was married to director/producer Kip Gowans from 1962 to 1970. The couple had two sons together.

As an onscreen actress, Valerie worked almost entirely on television, appearing in a wide range of series from crime shows like *Vendetta* to the soap opera *Emergency Ward-10* and many historical dramas. She played Elizabeth Tudor *in Thursdays Theatre's* production of *The Young Elizabeth*, with actress Katharine Blake, who would play her mother in *Anne of the Thousand Days*, in the role of Mary Boleyn. The few films Valerie made include the historical crime drama *Nine Hours to Rama* (1963) co-starring Horst Buchholtz and José Ferrer, as well as the 1965 sci-fi *Invasion*.

Valerie Gearon only acted for a few more years after Anne of the Thousand Days was released. Her last role was in the series *Crown Court* (1974). She died in 2003 at the age of 65.

≈≈≈≈≈

Michael Johnson was convincing in the role of Anne Boleyn's sensitive and genteel brother George Boleyn. The relationship between these two siblings was, at the time, and still is, a source of much speculation because of the incestuous adultery accusation levied against them. Considering this claim was used, along with other highly contested stories of adultery, as grounds for arresting Anne and trying her for treason, it is very likely that this was a charge trumped up by Henry VIII in his effort to get rid of Anne. The film goes with the assumption that there was no incest between Anne and George.

Born in Grimsby, Lincolnshire, England in 1939, Michael Johnson had amassed considerable experience on television prior to *Anne of the Thousand Days* and was yet another cast mate who had costarred in *The Young Elizabeth*, several years earlier. Michael played the role of Elizabeth Tudor's love interest Robert Dudley. However, unlike the other actors portraying members the Boleyn family, Michael did very little historical drama before *Anne*. He was best known for crime series like *The Expert* and for TV dramas such as *The Newcomers*.

Michael Johnson was frequently seen on British television series throughout the 1970s and early 80s, including episodes of *The Shadow of the Tower* and *Juliet Bravo*. He died in 2001 at the age of 61.

≈≈≈≈≈

Gary Bond played music teacher Mark Smeaton, whose false confession to adultery with Anne was so memorably tortured out of him by Cromwell's henchman. Gary played this tricky scene as well as the trial scene very effectively. He is likable and sympathetic as the kindly, innocent palace music tutor who is unjustly dragged into Henry's battle with Anne. His distress, both physical and emotional, comes across as very real to the audience, provoking deep pity and outrage.

Born in Liss Hampshire, England in 1940, the dashing actor/singer Gary Bond received his training at the Central School of Speech and Drama, which he attended on a scholarship. Although one of his early roles was as Private Cole in the big screen historical war drama *Zulu*, Gary soon became a prolific TV actor, appearing in many series between 1964-1969, including several episodes of *Great Expectations*, and *Frontier*.

The same year he did *Anne of the Thousand Days*, he was in an episode of the classic spy series *The Avengers*. He also worked extensively in the theater and would eventually have huge success playing the title role in *Joseph and the Amazing Technicolor Dreamcoat*. Shortly after *Anne* was released, Gary played one of his most memorable film roles, John Grant, in the Australian thriller *Wake in Fright*. He worked steadily in TV drama until 1990. He died in 1995 at the age of 55.

≈≈≈≈≈

Among the most accomplished supporting actors cast in *Anne of the Thousand Days* was William Squire, who played the relatively small but important role of Thomas More. The biggest and most far-reaching consequence of Henry VIII's annulment from Katherine of Aragon was his break from the Roman Catholic Church, resulting in the Protestant based Church of England with the monarch as its leader.

There were multitudes of people who refused to swear allegiance to this new faith. More, a lawyer and statesman, who was eventually venerated Saint Thomas More, is the most celebrated martyr from this chapter of history, and William does not disappoint in his depiction of him, playing More with sincerity, humility and dignity.

William Squire was born in Neath, Glamorgan, Wales, in 1916. His second wife was actress Juliet Harmer. William had notable experience on both the big and small screen, acting in many historical dramas, including adaptations of literary classics. He was also a prominent stage actor and starred on Broadway. In 1962 William replaced his friend Richard Burton in the role of King Arthur in *Camelot*. The two actors were frequent costars. Before *Anne*, they worked together in the films *Alexander the Great* and *Where Eagles Dare*.

William was in demand during the next two decades, with roles in popular TV series like *Doctor Who* and *The Black Arrow*. On the big screen he voiced Gandalf for the 1978 animated adaptation of *Lord of the Rings*. He died 1989 at the age of 73.

≈≈≈≈≈

Nicola Pagett played Princess Mary, destined to be Queen Mary I of England, very convincingly. Naturally regal in look and manner, Nicola was well cast and her performance as Katherine of Aragon's fiercely loyal daughter at her mother's deathbed was very moving. She is another example of an *Anne of the Thousand Days* cast member who made a memorable impression with her brief time onscreen.

Born in Cairo, Egypt as Nicola Scott in 1945, the striking actress grew up mainly in Japan and Hong Kong, because of her father's work. After attending Catholic boarding school in the UK, as a teenager, she chose to enroll in the prestigious Royal Academy of Dramatic Art, instead of going on to a Swiss finishing school. She had a daughter with her husband Graham Swannell. The marriage lasted from 1975 to 1998.

Nicola appeared in a number of mystery and spy dramas on TV prior to *Anne*. One of her few movie roles during this period was as Talia in the intriguing 1967 adventure *The Viking Queen*. Within a few years after *Anne*, she would go on to greater fame playing Elizabeth Bellamy in small screen hit *Upstairs, Downstairs*.

Directing History: Charles Jarrott

A sweeping costume epic such as *Anne of the Thousand Days* is an ambitious big screen endeavor for any director, but Charles Jarrott, despite little feature film experience, more than succeeded in the task of helming this high profile Hal B. Wallis production.

Charles Jarrott was born in London, England on June 16, 1927 to early racecar driver turned businessman Charles Jarrott O.B.E. and musical-comedy performer Violet Aline St Clair-Erskine (née Vyner) Countess of Rosslyn.

 When Charles was just 16-years-old his father died. Soon after losing his father, he convinced his mother to let him join the Royal Navy during World War II, and was stationed in the Far East.

The young man took after Charles Jarrott Sr. when it came to his integrity and determination, which may have accounted for Charles' eagerness to join the fight for his country in the war, at such a tender age. However, his interest in and aptitude for the entertainment industry, likely inherited from his mother, would quickly become apparent.

Soon after his military service, Charles went into show business, working as an actor/director/stage manager for the Nottingham Repertory Theatre. He married his first wife Rosemary Palin in 1949. They divorced in 1957.

The upper class Brit had a polished but affable demeanor. He was sensitive, thoughtful and easygoing; all qualities that could only help when it came to dealing with temperamental actors, and the stress of directing a project on stage or screen.

Charles Jarrott's career began to gain momentum in the 1950s after he moved to Canada and directed his first televised play, *Trial Balance*, for the Canadian Broadcasting Corporation. This was also the first of many small screen collaborations he would have with the cutting edge Canadian producer, Sydney Newman, who supported originality. It was around this time that he married his second wife, actress Katharine Blake, who was six years his senior. The union gave him two stepdaughters and the marriage lasted from 1959 to 1982.

Charles would again work with Sydney Newman, after he went back to the UK in 1960 and became a part of Newman's team of young directors. Over the next few years Charles would direct episodes of many series, in a wide range of genres, including suspense shows such as *Armchair Mystery Theatre*. Some of his most prominent shows were TV adaptations of two Harold Pinter plays.

In addition to mystery, fantasy and literary classics, the versatile filmmaker also gained experience with historical drama. He directed a 1964 episode of *Festival*, titled *The Life of Galileo*, and for *Thursday Theatre* the episode *The Young Elizabeth*, featuring several of the actors who he would go on to work with in *Anne of the Thousand Days*, including his wife, Katharine Blake.

He also directed teleplays written by Katharine, including an episode of *The Wednesday Play* in 1966 titled *The Snow Ball*, in which she also starred, and the first installment of the 1967 miniseries *Haunted* titled *To Blow My Name About*. During this period, *The Wednesday Play* had a reputation for giving up-and-coming directors, as well as writers, the opportunity to hone their craft. Charles likely benefited from this, as he directed five episodes of the series.

When asked in later years if his experience as a television director helped or hurt when he started directing films, Charles said that he didn't think there was much difference between directing the two mediums but that directing TV series did help him to gain experience dealing with various types of actors and stories.

Although his legacy would be in his work as a director, Charles did not completely give up his acting career when he started working behind the camera. He continued acting on stage after moving to Canada and began to appear onscreen in the 1950s, when he played many roles ranging from doctors to lawyers to soldiers in episodes of several TV drama series. Additionally, he produced a number of episodes of the same series he directed and would later do some screenwriting.

In the late 1960s, just before production on *Anne*, Charles directed several TV movies including a popular adaptation of *The Strange Case of Dr. Jekyll and Mr. Hyde*, starring Jack Palance, who was praised for his compelling depiction of the lead. The small screen project was so well received, it rivaled the earlier feature film versions.

By 1969, Charles had only directed one feature film, the 1962 crime drama *Time to Remember*, but Hal B. Wallis, once again displaying his amazing instincts and visionary skills, saw the potential in Charles for success on a grand scale. Considering the time, effort and care Wallis had invested in *Anne of the Thousand Days*, in the years leading up to the filming to ensure that it was a high quality production, he must have been very impressed with this TV director to trust him with such an important project.

Whether Wallis knew it or not, Charles' personality was one of his greatest assets when it came to directing a picture like this. The soft-spoken, laid-back director would have been well-suited to deal with this cast, especially the willful and passionate Richard Burton, who was there under duress. An aggressive or combative filmmaker would've been disastrous on this set, with so many strong personalities and big egos.

Charles was labeled a "woman's director" because of the great performances he got out of his actresses, including Geneviève's splendid portrayal of Anne Boleyn. His gift for bringing out the best in actresses may be one reason Geneviève was able to dominate the film to the extent that she did. Charles himself attributed his success in this area to the enjoyment he had for working with women and speculated that it also had something to do with the fact that he did not go in for male-female game playing.

He seemed to have a lot of respect for women, which in itself, would have gone a long way with the women he directed, particularly during this era when chauvinism was still so prevalent. Having a mother who had a background on the stage probably helped to shape his attitude toward actresses, in general. In an interview with Austin TV personality Carolyn Jackson, he pointed out how prominent female stars were in the 1930s and 40s, and thought women should again be given equal screen time.

Anne of the Thousand Days has been criticized for its slow pace and staginess. Critic Pauline Kael accused Charles of lacking style and personality. While it's true that we are not likely to hear references like "Charles Jarrott style film" or "Jarrottesque" thrown around, this does not mean the director didn't have his own personal style. But he was clearly not on a mission to get attention for himself and put his own distinctive mark all over the movie, as a more ego-driven filmmaker might. Charles' directing was subtle, unpretentious.

It was virtually free of gimmicks or showiness, which may be disappointing for some. However, a simple straightforward style of directing was refreshing, maybe even necessary due to the abundance of pageantry, opulent visuals, rich music and melodrama.

Typically, it is not good for the director's technique to really stand out because when we notice something like this, it interferes with the suspension of reality. Ideally, we should be able to forget we are watching a film, so that we can get swept up in the story and action on screen, which happens easily enough with *Anne of the Thousand Days*. But if you make a conscious decision to observe how the movie is directed, the logic and common sense behind most of the decisions Charles made is obvious.

Charles saved the dramatic shots for where they were most needed, often as the opening shots of important scenes, which makes them all the more powerful. His understated approach was also effective in that it allowed the film to have a more natural atmosphere and rapport between the actors, which is unusual for this particular genre but is beneficial to *Anne of the Thousand Days* because it reminds us that these characters are based on real people. We can relate to them more easily than characters depicted in similar epics, who often come across as historical figures rather than flesh and blood humans. It is essential to personalize Henry and Anne's story as much as possible because this is basically a romance, albeit a very tragic one.

There's no denying *Anne* is a film full of dynamic performances and Charles Jarrott's impact should not be discounted, especially when it comes to Geneviève

Bujold, who would've depended on his guidance more than the veteran actors, since this was her first big, international picture.

When awards season rolled around, Charles Jarrott was snubbed by the Academy of Motion Picture Arts and Sciences, while the film itself was nominated for Best Picture. It is somewhat of a contradiction for the director of a Best Picture nominee to not receive a nomination, which happened again with the follow-up *Mary, Queen of Scots* a couple of years later.

In the case of *Anne*, there could be a number of reasons for this slight. This was one of Charles' very first feature films, so maybe there were too many voters who felt he hadn't yet earned the right to be up for an Oscar, or it could've been due to show business politics, or the influence of the critics. He did win the prestigious Golden Globe award for *Anne of the Thousand Days*, which must have been some consolation.

Charles went on to direct *Mary, Queen of Scots* (1971) for Hal Wallis. One of his best known projects after *Anne*, was the 1976 feature film adaptation of Sidney Sheldon's famous novel, *The Other Side of Midnight*. He mainly worked in television in the years that followed, directing many TV movies about public figures including the memorable *Poor Little Rich Girl: The Barbara Hutton Story*, starring Farrah Fawcett.

After divorcing Katharine Blake in 1982, he married his third wife, Suzanne Bledsoe in 1992. The marriage lasted until her death in 2003. Charles Jarrott died in 2011 at the age of 83.

New Friendships and Old Rivalries

Although Richard Burton generally had a favorable opinion of John Colicos and Anthony Quayle, as actors, he could be critical but did admit that they were well cast in their respective roles. He drew comparisons between Anthony Quayle and his character, the conniving Cardinal Thomas Wolsey. But he said that John Colicos differed from his character, Thomas Cromwell, in this respect, having heard that the actor was nice in his personal life. However, he did find him painfully boring to act with, claiming once that he was going to need al least a half a bottle of vodka to get through an entire day of working with him. To put things in perspective, we must remember that Richard was very easily bored.

Richard had previously worked with John more than ten years earlier when they had appeared together in a *The DuPont Show of the Month* TV adaptation of *Wuthering Heights* in which Richard starred as Heathcliff, and John played Hindley. Richard did not remember working with him but Charles Jarrott reminded him before they reunited on *Anne of the Thousand Days*, so Richard was able to feign remembrance when he saw him again.

The fact that Richard personally knew so many of his castmates before filming began wasn't all good. He acknowledged that there was some bad blood between Anthony Quayle and himself but did not anticipate this as being a problem, thinking that Anthony would at least put up the pretense of friendship toward him. As he had predicted, Anthony was all smiles from the start.

A couple of months into filming, Anthony Quayle surprised Richard by revealing that he had spent part of his childhood in Pontypridd in Wales.

During the course of this shoot, Richard was surprised to suddenly realize how smart Anthony Quayle was, and at his extensive knowledge of poetry. Richard was not easy to impress when it came to intellectual capability, so Anthony must have come across as exceedingly brainy to earn his commendation in this area.

Richard was much kinder to Anthony, in his diary, toward the end of filming than he was at the beginning, when his attitude was still colored by past experience with the actor. He praised him for making the Stratford theater so popular, years earlier, by bringing such future icons as Laurence Olivier, Vivien Leigh, John Gielgud and others there.

Richard also speculated that maybe Anthony had mellowed over the years. Assuming this was true, it could be part of the reason they seemed to get along better than one would expect during filming.

Richard surmised that he and Elizabeth had had a bad influence on John Colicos, blaming their combined arrogance, money and fame for John developing his own inflated ego and a drinking problem, as well.

John Colicos himself admitted that he thought Richard was exciting and that he inspired excitement within other people. When he and his wife, Mona McHenry, had an argument during this period, because she noticed he kept using words completely unfamiliar to her and that he had a totally different attitude, John blamed Richard. Considering how articulate Richard was, it's easy to see how spending so much time in his presence could have had an effect on John's vocabulary.

Richard said, in his diary, that John had convinced himself that he was his equal when it came to his appeal as an actor, and that John felt his wife should be as appealing as Elizabeth. According to Richard, John had lost an upcoming film role due to his behavior, and Richard implied that his wife had left him, but the couple was actually married until 1981.

While it's true that Richard and Elizabeth influenced countless people, including many they never even met, Richard's own ego may have led him to over-exaggerate the impact he had on the actor. After all, John was no impressionable youth at this point; he was a 40-year-old actor with a long resume of credits behind him and years of experience with celebrities.

However, it is obvious that there was some change in him during this time, because Richard implied that John had turned off everyone else to the point where he was alone in his sympathy for the actor. If John Colicos really did become arrogant and overbearing during filming, it may have had something to do with the fact that he finally had a prominent role in a very high profile film, quite a departure from the obscure films and TV series that he was known for up until then.

Reports from the Set

We are fortunate to have not only recollections from cast and production staff, as to the *Anne of the Thousand Days* shoot, but information that was recorded during filming itself, such as entries in Richard Burton's diaries at the time, and on-set interviews. Much can be gleaned from these sources as to the atmosphere of the set, the approach of the actors and filmmakers, and onset relationships. We see how this movie succeeded because of, or in some cases in spite of, what was happening behind-the-scenes.

It was on the set of another period film, centering on a love-hate relationship, the 1967 Franco Zeffirelli adaptation of William Shakespeare's *The Taming of the Shrew*, starring Richard and Elizabeth, that Wallis discussed plans for *Anne of the Thousand Days* during a memorable lunch with the two iconic actors. Wallis was struck by the opulence of the couple's private quarters at the Cinecitta Studios in Italy and their self-indulgent attitude during the very long, sumptuous luncheon in which the stars kept ignoring the efforts of Franco Zeffirelli and the assistant directors to get them back on the set.

Wallis was surprised by how attentive Elizabeth was, while listening to him talk about the project, considering she didn't have a part in the production. But he went from surprised to stupefied when she finally revealed why she was so interested in the forthcoming movie. The actress, who would be 37-years-old by the time filming began in 1969, was very anxious to play the part of Anne, who was only supposed to be 22-years-old at the beginning of the story. In addition to the age difference, she was a different type physically. She was much more voluptuous than Anne Boleyn had been.

Her announcement that she must play Anne caused Wallis to freeze, with his fork in the air. The producer was suddenly in a very awkward position but Richard swooped in and, as he looked her in the eye, put his hand over hers and apologetically told Elizabeth she was too old for the role. To her credit, she handled the rejection very well, in the moment.

In light of Elizabeth's disappointment at being refused the role of Anne Boleyn, Richard tried to get out of playing Henry. It was the possibility of being sued by Universal that prompted him to go through with it.

If you believe Hal Wallis' side of the story, Richard had initially begged for the role of Henry. Whatever his feelings may have been in the beginning, by the time filming was about to get underway, Richard had soured on the project, to say the least.

There seem to be a number of reasons for his change in attitude. Besides resentment over Elizabeth being passed over for the part of Anne, he was extremely critical of the script, could not get excited about the prospect of playing Henry VIII, and was going through a difficult time in his life.

Not only had Elizabeth, who was plagued by health issues over the years, undergone a hysterectomy and traumatic recovery the year before, but was now suffering from apparently severe hemorrhoids, which necessitated treatments at a hospital. However, the most discouraging thing of all may have been the fact that both he and Elizabeth had become disenchanted by moviemaking and were seriously considering retirement.

One reason Richard wanted to stop acting was because he found it boring, not just in films but the stage as well. It stands to reason that a mind as sharp and active as Richard's would be in need a lot of stimulation, and boredom at work could be a real problem for him.

He was even concerned about the possibility of being bored by Genevieve Bujold or director Charles Jarrott. But as hard as it was for Richard to cope with boredom, one of his worst fears was that he would come across as boring to others. One night when he was trying to stay away from alcohol, a barb from Elizabeth about how dull he was when he was sober, prompted him to drink 23 shots of straight tequila, chased with a few bottles of Carta Blanca beer.

Richard was also worried about whether he would like and get along with Geneviève, remembering the bad times he had with a couple of his previous leading ladies: Lana Turner, and more recently Mary Ure. Richard also had concerns over his own performance. He made up his mind that his character was insane and evil, while at the same time acknowledging his charm and cynical but superior intellect.

However, he did hold out hope that maybe be could do something with the project, seeing even more potential, provided both his leading lady and the director did a good job.

When he first arrived, Richard had costume fittings, a chore which he loathed, and later did a read-through with the entire cast. Richard had predicted that the read-through would be rough on Geneviève, in the presence of such seasoned professionals; and hearing her describe it years later, it does appear she was rather awe-struck.

Anthony Quayle was very careful and precise in the reading of his part when the cast did the initial read-through. John Colicos read his lines with a noticeably resonant voice. Richard observed that both Quayle and Colicos read in an extremely theatrical style; and this prompted Richard to read his part in a rough voice and at a fast pace, so as to differentiate himself from them.

Richard was concerned hearing Geneviève read her part, the first time, that she might have a problem delivering lengthy speeches but thought this could be remedied in the editing room by cutting to shots of the other actors in the scene and also with a little dubbing.

Geneviève possessed the enthusiasm for her part in the film that Richard lacked for his, and why not? Anne Boleyn is not always depicted as a heroine in the cinema but she was in this film; and the character was a challenging one, particularly for an actress in the early phase of her career.

In a interview conducted during the shoot, Geneviève revealed that she had read a lot about Anne Boleyn and loved her. She wanted to bring Anne to life and make her as contemporary as she could.

This was also a golden opportunity for Geneviève to become an international star; whereas Richard was at a very different place in his life and career with little to gain from the movie, apart from his impressive salary and perhaps another Oscar-nomination. But the chances of the oft-nominated actor actually taking home one of the coveted statuettes must have appeared slim at this point.

Hal Wallis' faith in the adaptation of *Anne of the Thousand Days* seemed apparent, when interviewed on the set. He talked about how the appeal of historic films was based on the fact that they dealt with history and that the captivating love story between Henry and Anne added to the appeal of this film, as well as the merit of the property itself, originating as a Maxwell Anderson play.

Wallis felt it was miraculous that he had found an actress so perfect for the role of Anne Boleyn. He proved to be a superb guide when it came to interpreting the character, which came as a surprise to Geneviève. He had also helped the actress to prepare by giving her multiple books to read on Anne Boleyn and hiring a coach to help her get the accent down. Wallis thought that Geneviève's French accent was an added benefit of casting her in the role, since Anne had been schooled at the French court, but he wanted to ensure the accent was chiefly British with a tinge of French.

Richard seemed very pleased to have his daughter Kate along, who at the age of 11 already seemed very interested in the production process, and was given a bit part in the film as a kitchen maid. It was the first movie role in what has turned out to be a long and distinguished career for Kate, who has not only been successful in film and TV but theater as well. Liza Todd, who was 11-years-old at the time, also had an uncredited cameo as a beggar maid.

Elizabeth Taylor's cameo takes place when she and a male companion, dressed for a masquerade, with their faces covered, run laughing into the palace chapel interrupting Katherine while she is at prayer. Discovering the queen in a very private moment, Elizabeth's character quickly bows out. Even in a disguise, Elizabeth Taylor lights up the screen, and not just because of all the glitter on her mask.

There were some lovely court dance sequences in the film and, early in the shoot, on May 29, Richard and Geneviève spent the morning working with two ballet dancers. He was out of his element and uncomfortable doing a style of dance that he seemed to view as effeminate, and admitted to some annoyance, blaming his macho background and growing up around miners for his attitude.

As early as May 31, another day when the two had to dance together, Richard, who speculated that she may have been on edge at this time, was already starting to grow weary and bored with Geneviève, according to his diary. It probably didn't help his attitude toward her that mentally, he continued to silently compare Geneviève with Elizabeth when it came to his co-star's suitability for the role, firmly believing Elizabeth would have been better, and that Geneviève would merely be adequate. He did, however, find Geneviève significantly more attractive by the beginning of production than he had at their first meeting in Paris.

He took note of how petite Geneviève was, overall, although the 5'4 actress bragged that she was still taller than Elizabeth Taylor, who was just over 5'0. Geneviève reminded Richard of Vivien Leigh because of her size and the fact that she was so pert. When Elizabeth heard him compare Geneviève to Vivien Leigh, it upset her because she herself had been compared to Leigh in the past, even being chosen to replace her in the film *Elephant Walk*, many years earlier.

One thing he seems to have liked about Geneviève was her bluntness. When they brought out the models of the set made from cardboard, Geneviève referred to them as dollhouses and said they didn't mean anything to her. Richard appreciated the remark and thought it sounded like something Elizabeth would say.

Richard already had confidence in his distinguished co-stars Michael Horderrn, John Colicos, and Anthony Quayle. He held Michael Hordern in particularly high regard, considering him to be one of the world's greatest actors, and challenging to play against, in that sharing the screen with him meant an actor had to be in top form in order to hold their own.

According to Terence Wilton, who played Lord Percy, Richard's acting was much admired on the set. Many years after making *Anne of the Thousand Days*, Wilton remembered how similar he was to Henry VIII. He said that the older actors in the cast would applaud his performance.

On May 21, Richard rehearsed the song *Farewell My Love* for the movie. He liked the song but found it challenging as an amateur, to learn on such short notice, because of the song's many stops and starts.

On May 23, Richard went to visit his brother Ivor, who had become incapacitated following an accident at Richard's house in Switzerland. Richard was annoyed that the drive from Shepperton Studios to where Ivor was staying turned out be much longer than he had been told. He phoned associate producer Richard McWhorter and explained that the working day would be nearly over, after he had visited Ivor for an hour and driven back to the studio. But McWhorter informed him that Charles Jarrott and Hal Wallis agreed that seeing Ivor was more important, so they had held rehearsals in his absence.

May 27 was the first day Richard actually enjoyed rehearsing the project. He thought it was because there were a number of other actors present besides Geneviève Bujold, Anthony Quayle and John Colicos. But Richard was self-conscious about the beard he had grown for the role, thinking he resembled Welsh Buccaneer Henry Morgan.

His make-up artist was going to work on his beard -- which had originally grown in several different colors -- and on his face to give him a more Tudorian look. However, Richard did not really try to look like Henry VIII. The absence of red hair, which so many other actors have donned for the role, was conspicuous in Richard's depiction.

Richard admitted that the roles he played influenced him in private life and said that playing Henry VIII had exaggerated his authoritarian streak. He would insist on paying the bill at lunch, sending people home in his car and picking up the tab for drinks. While this may have seemed a bit overbearing, Henry's pomposity was surely not the worst characteristic of the tyrannical king that Richard could have picked up. But Richard had struggled to formulate his interpretation of Henry and ended up playing him, as mainly an extension of his own personality.

Geneviève would later tell author Susan Bordo that it's not possible to put something into a character you're playing that doesn't exist within yourself. Fortunately, for the actress, and the film itself, this character felt very natural to her and she was able to identify with Anne right away. She also knew that Wallis had seen something of Anne in her when he cast her in the role, which must have been assuring, but she definitely had her own challenges along the way. Anne Boleyn's English dialogue was unfamiliar to Geneviève, who hadn't learned to speak English until she was 18, and had been trained in French-Canadian theater.

She had learned something about acting from her time with the filmmaker Alain Resnais, that stuck with her. He had taught Geneviève to carry through to the end of a movement, and that she should let the character fully expand. The actress saw this same sense of commitment in Anne herself, and we see a strong commitment to the character in Geneviève's performance.

Although Richard was not known for having an easy-going disposition, he seemed particularly peevish around the time *Anne of the Thousand Days* was in production. There were probably a number of reasons for this, including his negative attitude toward the film, and the stress he was under due to Elizabeth's health concerns. His decision to cut down on alcohol during this period, with the intention of quitting, was probably another factor in his irritability.

Often a charming rogue, who could be the life of the party on movie sets, Richard, according to his own admission, had become more and more anti-social over the past year or longer and could only loosen up when he was rather drunk.

On May 31, Richard's friend Tim Hardy visited the Kalizma. Hardy was a descendent of Richard III, who of course, was Henry VIII's maternal uncle, and had been usurped by Henry's father at The Battle of Bosworth Field. Hardy informed him of what a great archer Henry was and demonstrated to Richard how he should go about it.

After finishing a lengthy scene with Geneviève on June 7, in which he had most of the lines, he had to do one with Anthony Quayle and Michael Hordern. In his diary Richard praised both actors for their skill and craftiness, each apparently vying for the audience's attention with clever mannerisms.

According to Richard, Hordern and Quayle, also played with their timing in this scene and the way they read their lines to throw off the other actors. But Richard felt this was something they were doing subconsciously, and he himself, got into the game. He said they were well aware that you had to look out for yourself when the camera is on. Richard pointed out that the star can be generous to other actors when it comes to things like this but he also felt the need to be on his toes, especially when working with real professionals like Quayle and Hordern.

Like Richard Burton, 43-year-old Greek actress Irene Papas, was another of the cast members who was questioning whether or not she wanted to continue her acting career at this time. When she was interviewed at Shepperton Studios in early July, by Roger Ebert while filming was underway on *Anne of the Thousand Days*, she admitted that she thought about retiring from acting, expressing the opinion that it's good to occasionally switch professions. She went on to compare acting to teaching, essentially saying it was the same thing, and that as one matures their desire to teach lessens.

Another reason she was considering changing careers was because she wanted to do something that she could put more of herself into, explaining that when she was acting she always allowed herself to be guided by the director even if it meant playing a scene differently than she wanted.

On the day of Roger Ebert's interview, Irene, who candidly talked about a wide range of subjects from politics to filmmaking, to philosophy and culture, was at the studio for costume fittings and she stopped by the set to watch the scene between Richard and Geneviève, in which Henry agrees to get rid of Katherine. She smilingly remarked to Ebert that she'd always personally preferred Anne Boleyn to Katherine of Aragon, reasoning that Katherine had already been married to Henry for 20 years, so why shouldn't another woman get a chance? But then told Ebert not to quote her, pointing out how the English loved Queen Katherine.

As they watched the scene, she recalled an audition she had done years earlier for a part opposite Richard Burton on the film *Alexander the Great*. She told Roger that she didn't get the role, explaining that she was never cast in parts she auditioned for because she didn't like the idea of being judged.

After the scene was finished Irene met her director Charles Jarrott for the first time. She also greeted Richard and Geneviève and Elizabeth Taylor's daughter

Liza, before heading to the studio commissary with Roger Ebert to finish their interview.

In mid-July when he had cut way down on his drinking, Richard was going through withdrawal, and talked in his diary about how difficult it was for him to get along with people, even those he highly respected. He was so bored with acting by this time, that he felt he had to drink in order to make it tolerable.

On July 29, the author and politician Sir Alan (A.P.) Herbert was a guest of Richard's for luncheon at the Dorchester Hotel. His granddaughter was playing a lady in waiting to Anne Boleyn in the film. Geneviève said that the 78-year-old made a pass at her but Richard had his doubts, speculating that it was wishful thinking on her part.

By the middle of August, Richard was totally bored with work on the film and really dreaded the coming weeks. During this time he was exceptionally critical of Geneviève in his diary, on several accounts. He was frustrated that the actress had not been persuaded by efforts of himself and his friends to believe in her own desirability.

He also complained about her frequenting discos with her husband, Paul Almond, and showing up for work looking and smelling terrible and continually vomiting. He didn't understand why she couldn't look wonderful, even on very little sleep, comparing her, unfavorably, yet again to the goddess at home, Elizabeth Taylor who could, he claimed, appear fresh-faced with as little as 15 minutes sleep. He also criticized Geneviève's parenting, accusing her of ignoring her small son Matthew.

Monday, August 11, Richard reflected on the recent heat and humidity, that day when they were supposed to film the scene where he and Geneviève were in bed together, predicting that it would be sweaty. When you think of the thick fur blankets covering them, it's easy to imagine the discomfort on a sticky August day such as that.

Although Elizabeth Taylor had a cameo in the film and she was married to the male lead, she made her presence scarce on the set, something that suited Hal Wallis just fine. He liked Elizabeth but was worried that she, or more specifically her jealousy, which had become quite clear, would have an impact on Geneviève's performance. However, timing is everything and it was probably no coincidence that, toward the end of production, Elizabeth showed up unexpectedly, her entourage in tow, just as they were about to film the Tower scene, a particularly demanding day for Geneviève.

In his memoir Wallis recounted how a furious Geneviève, about to take her place before the camera, turned to Charles Jarrott and himself and, referring to Elizabeth as a bitch, said she was going to give her an acting lesson she would never forget. It turned out to be an acting lesson none of us would forget. And so, it appears that the fire Genevieve displays in that iconic scene was very real, which would mean that Elizabeth contributed something more powerful to the film than her brief cameo as a masked courtier.

It was obvious to Hal Wallis that Elizabeth's visit had turned out to be blessing in disguise, and he noted in his memoir that he had rarely seen an actor, over the course of his career, match the skill that Geneviève demonstrated that day. And this was a man who had worked with many of the biggest and most prestigious screen stars of all time. As soon as she had delivered this unforgettable performance, Geneviève made a dramatic exit by storming off the set.

One of the most important scenes was the most tragic, and in complete contrast to the romantic storyline that carried the majority of the film, the beheading of Anne Boleyn. In an interview on the set, Charles Jarrott explained that Anne's execution was unusual and described the way they attempted to recreate it on screen.

Jarrott talked about how, typically, the doomed person climbs a scaffold, kneels, says a prayer, and then the blade is raised and comes down to sever their head. Anne's execution was different because she was beheaded by a swordsman and she looked up at him when he raised his hand. The swordsman, who happened to be from France, told his assistant, in French to distract her, which the assistant did by walking in front of her. When she turned to look at the assistant the executioner lowered the sword.

Jarrott acknowledged the crudeness of the moment, explaining that they wanted to capture that, along with the horrid aspect of the event instead of presenting a tidy version of the execution.

On August 21, Richard was glad that there was only more week of filming to go. As the production drew to a close, Michael Hordern threw a party. Richard was surprised that Michael would start the party at 9p.m. since it was necessary for the guest in the film industry to get up early. When filming was completed the customary wrap party was thrown, but it was a divided evening, with Elizabeth and Geneviève each holding court at opposite ends of the room and Richard remaining by Elizabeth's side.

A work by William Hogarth circa 1728
titled King Henry the Eighth and Anna Bullen
William Hogarth [CC0]
Wikimedia Commons

Queen Elizabeth
A sketch of Elizabeth I
Federico Zuccari [Public domain]
Wikimedia Commons

Photograph of (from left) Maxwell Anderson,
S. N. Behrman, Robert E. Sherwood and Elmer Rice,
four of the five founders of the Playwrights' Company

Stage Publishing Company, Inc., photograph by Alfredo Valente
[Public domain]

Publicity Photo of Genevieve Bujold for *Anne of the Thousand Days*
movie studio [Public domain]

Elizabeth Taylor and Richard Burton (1965)
Wikimedia Commons
Joop van Bilsen / Anefo [CC0]

Georges Delerue, composer of the film's music
Wikimedia Commons
https://creativecommons.org/licenses/by-sa/3.0/deed.en

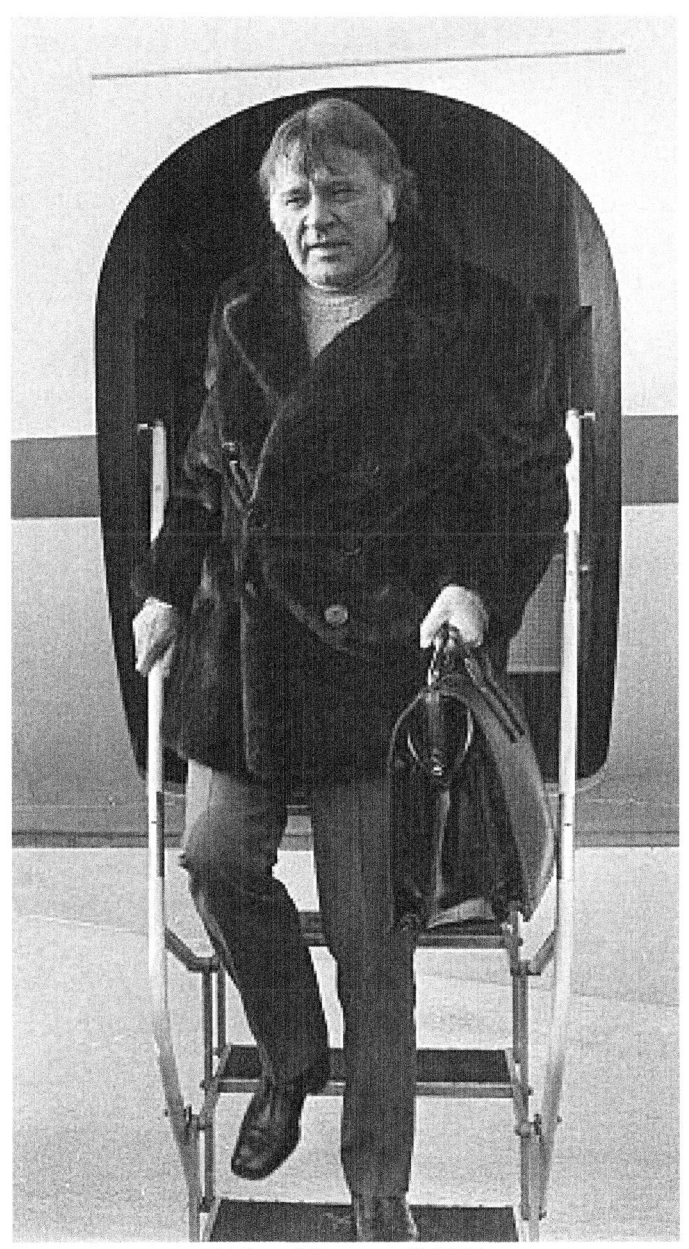

Richard Burton (1971)

Anefo / Mieremet, R. [CC BY-SA 3.0 nl (https://creativecommons.org/licenses/by-sa/3.0/nl/deed.en)]creativecommons.org/licenses/by-sa/3.0/nl/deed.en

Henry & Anne & Richard & Geneviève

Many people take it for granted that there was a behind-the-scenes romance between Richard Burton and Geneviève Bujold, during and perhaps after the filming of *Anne of the Thousand Days*. According to *The Daily Mail* this alleged affair started when Elizabeth Taylor had to stay in the hospital to be treated for piles. The fact that they were both married to other people at the time offers little if any cause for doubt, considering Richard was a serial adulterer, and Geneviève admitted that she left her husband, Paul Almond, because she fell in love with another man.

Whether or not there is any truth in the widespread rumors about Richard and Geneviève, we have a long list of reasons to find it believable in our minds. There was definite chemistry between the two. They were both very attractive, charismatic and sexy. Richard was going through a difficult time in his marriage to Elizabeth and although the couple enjoyed a legendarily passionate relationship, they had been together for about seven years by this time.

Geneviève, who had yet to achieve worldwide fame at this point, was in awe of Richard Burton. But one of the most compelling reasons to believe the gossip, is that they were co-stars working closely together, portraying lovers. There have been so many actors involved in on-set romances over the years, it is almost an automatic assumption, when there is any sexual chemistry, that the real action is happening between takes.

Geneviève would one day remember with humor, that the idea of reading love scenes with Richard Burton was terrifying to her. This discomfort really isn't surprising under the circumstances. Not only was he a huge star, but nearly 17 years older than her. He was a romantic matinee idol onscreen and a Casanova off screen.

Any such romance would have had a number of things in common with the relationship of Henry VIII and Anne Boleyn. Like the characters they were playing, there was a substantial age difference between Richard and Geneviève. The two actors were both regarded as being very intense in real life, like their characters, which could have resulted in a great love affair. Richard, toward the end of filming, made a point of vilifying Geneviève in the pages of his diary, similar to the anti-Anne propaganda that was largely orchestrated, it would seem, either by Henry VIII or his henchmen, shortly before her arrest.

In *The Richard Burton Diaries* the actor insists that he did not betray Elizabeth's trust, but says she would not believe him. He makes mysterious references to Geneviève's behavior upsetting them in some way, and speculates that maybe it was her intention. He criticizes her for being ambitious and talks about how much people dislike her, saying he was the one who saw to it that she was treated like a star and that people socialized with her out of loyalty to him.

Because of his vagueness, there are various ways that his words can be interpreted but the image of a scheming opportunist, not unlike the perception many still have of Anne Boleyn, jumps off the page.

However, these particular entries should be read with a fair amount of skepticism and are perceived by some as nothing more than a cover. We know that Elizabeth was privy to Richard's diaries, she even wrote in them herself on occasion. If it was true that he and Geneviève were having a secret affair, it would have been idiotic for him to admit it in writing, especially in a journal that was so easily accessible to his wife, although it would make total sense to use such a diary to disparage Geneviève's character and to proclaim his own innocence.

Geneviève does not address the rumors that she and Richard Burton had an affair but, in contrast to the negative way he described her in his diary, she seems to only have kind words in reminiscing about him. She has, however, said that she and Richard went their separate ways when the film wrapped, which contradicts reports that they had a long relationship.

Apparently, unsure of exactly what happened between the two actors, Hal Wallis ventured that it may have gone no farther than playful flirting. But Elizabeth took the matter very seriously. Although she was hardly ever on the set, she did her best to keep tabs on Richard, continually calling to check up on him and wanting to know when he would be home.

Elizabeth Taylor may have been the queen of Hollywood during her time but unlike Henry VIII's first queen consort Katherine of Aragon, she was far from saintly. Elizabeth had been the other woman, herself, more than once, so it's only natural that she would be suspicious of Richard and Geneviève, especially since her own affair with him had led to the breakup of his marriage to Sybil.

Elizabeth was particularly concerned when Richard began referring to Geneviève as "Gin". This was seen as a red flag, because in the past, he only nicknamed an actress if he was sleeping with her. Speculation from the press that the two costars were having an affair probably didn't make things any easier, but it was almost inevitable that there would be such gossip, considering the fact that it had been several years since Richard had an onscreen love interest other than Elizabeth. Add to this Geneviève's beauty and youth and Richard's history of adultery and it just makes sense that many people would assume their offscreen relationship was not platonic.

Even if there was truth in the gossip surrounding the two co-stars, the consequences of any relationship they might have had was nothing compared to the far-reaching ramifications of what happened between the lovers they were playing on screen. The mere possibility that there may have been an adulterous romance between Richard and Geneviève is enough to capture our imaginations. With that in mind, perhaps it is best that we don't know, for sure, but are left to wonder if the passion they projected in their scenes together was real.

Dressing Up

The costumes in some period films are more memorable than others, but with *Anne of the Thousand Days*, the costumes were not only gorgeous but really like another character in the film. It's hard to imagine the actors in this film, especially Geneviève Bujold, dressed in anything other than these exquisite creations. In addition to being a feast for our eyes, these decadent garments with their rich sumptuous fabrics and ornate details, play a big part in bringing Henry VIII's lavish 16th century Royal court to life on screen.

The main person responsible for the wardrobe we see in *Anne of the Thousand Days* was the very accomplished costume designer Margaret Furse. She was born in London, England as Alice Margaret Watts on February 18, 1911, to the well-known *Punch* magazine illustrator Arthur G. Watts and his wife Phyllis Gordon Watts. She married production and costume designer Roger K. Furse in 1936, which led to her career designing costumes in the theater and eventually for films.

Margaret's first screen credit was as assistant to her husband Roger Furse when he did the costumes for Laurence Olivier's *Henry V* (1944). She and Roger later teamed up on another famous Olivier project, 1955's *Richard III*.

Margaret and Roger eventually divorced and she married Stephen Watts, (no relation to Margaret's family). However, she remained friendly with Roger and a lovely watercolor painting he did of Margaret during their marriage hangs in the primary collection of Britain's National Portrait Gallery in London.

Although she worked on many contemporary films, Margaret became very experienced at designing costumes for historical dramas, including: *Oliver Twist* (1948) the Victorian melodrama *Madeleine* (1950) and later historical epics like Hal B. Wallis' *Becket* (1964) and *The Lion in Winter* (1968). She had a particular flair for creating the kind of elegant and stunningly regal costumes needed for films set in royal courts, which made her an obvious choice to design for *Anne of the Thousand Days*.

Although Margaret Furse had already been nominated for three Oscars by 1969, and she had a big influence on the next generation of costume designers, Richard Burton was very critical of her. He highly praised the costumes, but was unimpressed with Margaret, giving the real credit to the two young men who sewed the garments. He claimed that Margaret completely depended on what she found in illustrated costume books and in pictures by Henry VIII's painter Hans Holbein.

Richard appreciated the fact that the costumers had chosen the lightest fabrics possible but judged the material to still be quite hot and predicted a lot of sweating in the months ahead. He also complained about the shape of his shoes. He had requested that they come up higher on the ankle, because he was self-conscious about the shape of his calves, but was denied because such shoes were not worn during that period.

Margaret may have sounded like a stickler for historical accuracy but there are critics today who accuse her of being somewhat loosey-goosey with details such as the shapes of sleeves and the size of the headdresses. Anne Boleyn is often credited with introducing the French hood to the Tudor court but there is evidence that Henry's sister Mary, Queen of France, was probably the first lady to bring this fashion to England. She is seen wearing one in a wedding portrait painted around 1516.

These rounded headdresses typically left the front of the hair uncovered and had a black veil attached at the back. They were a substitute for the gabled hood, which was angular and covered more of the head. Geneviève Bujold sports exaggerated versions of the French hood in many of the scenes from *Anne of the Thousand Days*. The height and very round shape have prompted some to compare it to a halo. It may seem a bit much to those who are familiar with the traditional French hood but the look is flattering to Geneviève's face.

Richard Burton may not have looked much like the image we have of Henry VIII but, thanks in part, to Margaret Furse and her staff he definitely looked the part of a king. Some of his costumes were so opulent and richly embellished they rivaled what any of the ladies wore, although, they were, for the most part masculine in style. The clothes extenuate Henry's bold outgoing nature and are also the garments of someone who is anxious to show off his status and wealth, which is typical of kings in general, and considering Henry's egotism, he was surely no exception.

Naturally, the supporting actors' costumes are much more subdued than those of the principal players, but many of these are eye catching as well, such as a green silk dress featuring sleeves with elaborate floral embroidery worn by Valerie Gearon. During Henry's visit to Heaver Castle, Michael Hordern and Katharine Blake are striking in simple but elegant matching gray his and hers ensembles. Even Irene Papas, who gives the appearance of being in perpetual mourning as the pious Katharine of Aragon, is a bit glamorous with sparkling gold trim added to her otherwise dark, matronly gowns.

Of course, the most exciting costumes featured in *Anne of the Thousand Days* were those worn by the leading lady, Geneviève Bujold, which is to be expected. Not only were her gowns exceptionally beautiful, but they were a good reflection of what was happening in Anne Boleyn's life at any given time.

At the beginning of the film, when Anne is a fresh young maiden, Geneviève is usually seen in simple girlish, pastel colored dresses. As her power and influence over Henry grows, so does the magnificence of her wardrobe. Soon we see her parading around in extravagant silk, satin, and velvet gowns.

These dazzling frocks are usually in vivid colors, like the sapphire gown she wears for the unforgettable scene in which the violent argument between her and Henry turns into a marriage proposal. The shimmering gold fabrics used for the underskirt of her deep brown dress and in the detail of her white coronation gown are effective in giving her a more regal appearance, befitting a woman of her grand status.

Georges Delerue's Haunting Soundtrack

Obviously, music can be a very important, or in some cases, an essential element in a film's success. The prolific, Oscar award-winning French composer Georges Delerue was aware of how powerful a motion picture score could be. He was a master of establishing a mood in a scene through the artistry of his music, which was his primary objective, rather than grinding out commercially popular theme songs. Creating music for the cinema, particularly, music that would enhance the quality of a movie was Delerue's goal in life and his passion.

Georges Henri Jean-Baptiste Delerue was born on March 12, 1925 in Roubaix, Nord, France, to a musical family. Music, which he began to study at the same time he was learning his alphabet, was a significant part of his childhood. Georges' mother enrolled him at the local music conservatory where he played the clarinet, later switching to piano. However, it would take a while for his enthusiasm for music to fully blossom.

During WWII he was forced to give up his studies, in order to help support his family by going to work in a factory. Scoliosis, complicated by injuries following a bicycle accident, necessitated an operation and convalescence of several months for the teenager. It was during this time of isolation that he became serious about music and embraced his destiny. Like a butterfly emerging from a cocoon, Georges came out of his confinement, transformed, from a young musician into a composer.

He was encouraged to compose for the screen early on, when he was a student at the Paris Conservatory, studying under Darius Milhaud and Henri Busser. He was at the conservatory on a scholarship but worked as a jazz pianist in Parisian bars in order to pay his expenses.

Georges was still in his twenties when he began conducting the Club d'Essai orchestra for French National Radio and Television. Additionally, he started to compose music for short films and for the stage, such as operas and ballets. As the 1950's came to a close he married Micheline Gautron, who had a child from a previous marriage. The couple would also have a daughter together named Claire.

By this time he was working with A-list movie directors, including Francois Truffaut, who was a frequent collaborator. Georges soon built up a prestigious reputation which put him in demand with American and British filmmakers. Some prominent feature films he scored, early in his career, include: *Hiroshima Mon Amour*; *Shoot the Piano Player*; and *Jules and Jim*.

A few years prior to *Anne of the Thousand Days*, Georges Delerue composed for the now classic historical drama *A Man for All Seasons*. The two films were similar in that they both dealt with Henry VIII's break with the Roman Catholic Church in order to divorce Katherine of Aragon to marry Anne Boleyn. However, *A Man for All Seasons* focused on Thomas More, and his decision to stand up to the king. Around this same time Georges did the music for what would be one of Geneviève Bujold's most popular films, *King of Hearts*. The year before *Anne of the Thousand Days* went into production, his music for the TV documentary *Our World* won an Emmy.

It was clear that a richly drawn royal court epic, full of high drama, would require an exceptional talent. to compose the music. So, Hal Wallis, who went to great lengths to ensure this would be a first rate production, signed Georges Delerue for the job.

According to Georges, himself, he did not know what he was going to write until he saw footage of the film. The images would awaken his creativity. It's easy to imagine how the cinematic adaptation of *Anne of the Thousand Days* directly inspired the music he wrote for it. Although in this case he did begin his work before the cameras started rolling in order to integrate the music with the production itself.

Listening to Georges' soundtrack one can't help but be struck by the melancholy quality that is present in so many of the pieces he composed. His gift for lovely melodies helps to bring out the bittersweet romance at the center of the film.

The chamber music style pieces had an important part in creating the atmosphere of a 16th century royal court. Wallis was very firm about using instruments from the period and this definitely added to authentic sound, especially tracks such as *Lute Song* as well as *Courts and Airs Dances*. The latter plays during the memorable scene at the beginning of the film, when Henry is first enchanted by Anne, as he sees her dance.

The crowning jewel of Georges' soundtrack is the haunting *Farewell My Love*, the strains of which can be heard throughout the film. Richard Burton, himself, sang the vocals for *Farewell My Love*. Richard admitted some difficulty in recording this challenging song, blaming his limitations as an amateur singer. However, considering this was after he had starred in the musical *Camelot* on Broadway for over a year, it would be a stretch to think of him as an amateur vocalist.

A distinct difference can be found in the theme music Georges Delerue composed for Henry as opposed to what he composed for Anne. Henry's theme runs a gamut of extremes: turbulent, pompous, sensitive, reflecting the moods of the king himself, while Anne's theme gradually follows her journey from fresh young maiden to a jaded and calculating queen.

As a composer of more than 350 movie and TV scores, music was his life and he thoroughly understood what an effective communication tool it could be. Despite his immense talent and many accolades, Georges was not the least bit arrogant, but was a surprisingly modest man, who remained focused on what was in the best interest of a film. His Oscar-nominated score for *Anne of the Thousand Days* is no exception. The music does not overshadow the action onscreen but complements the film. It is an ideal accompaniment for the beautiful visuals, Tudor England setting, and the tragic love story.

World Premiere and Awards Season

Anne of the Thousand Days had its U.S. premiere on December 18, 1969. Earlier in the month the film had been screened for the New York and Los Angeles press, who responded very enthusiastically according to Ed Henry of Universal who sent Richard Burton a telegram letting him know how well received it had been. Henry even went so far as to rank *Anne* above *Lion in Winter* and *A Man for All Seasons*. Richard was cautiously optimistic that the movie would turn out to be a big hit. He had a considerable stake in the project, beyond his reputation, since his contract gave him a substantial percentage of the profits.

The film's reception was generally positive but definitely had its share of negative reviews. Some critics felt that the movie's pace was more like a stage production than a film. This is common among film adaptations of plays, although in some cases it works surprisingly well.

Anne of the Thousand Days was sometimes panned as pompous and dull while being celebrated for its beauty, and juicy subject matter. One thing most reviewers could agree on was that the film featured wonderful performances particularly from Richard Burton and breakout star Geneviève Bujold.

In his diary on December 12, 1969, Richard talked about the possibility that Geneviève might win the Oscar, if she kept her negative opinions about Hollywood to herself. He went on to accuse her of being conceited, speculating that she considered herself to be the next Sarah Bernhardt.

Under the circumstances, Geneviève's Oscar nomination did not come as a huge surprise to her. She thought *Anne of the Thousand Days* turned out beautifully and that she, along with the other actors, did a good job. She explained to *The Montreal Gazette* that anyone but a fool would know you have a chance of being nominated, if you're good, and you are acting opposite Richard Burton in a Hal Wallis production.

There was heavy campaigning for the film leading up to awards season, with Universal putting a lot of money into promotion. *Time* speculated that its 10 Oscar nominations were due to wining and dining Academy members at 35 special screenings in which champagne and beef stroganoff were served. Richard and Elizabeth did their share of promotion as well, both of them going to Hollywood and attending events; Elizabeth agreeing to be a presenter at the Oscars, things which columnist Liz Smith implied were done to help Richard's chances of winning.

The film was nominated for Oscars in the following categories: Best Picture, **Hal B. Wallis;** Best Actor in a Leading Role, **Richard Burton;** Best Actress in a Leading Role, **Geneviève Bujold;** Best Actor in a Supporting Role, **Anthony Quayle;** Best Music (Original Score -- for a Motion Picture [Not a Musical]), **Georges Delerue;** Best Writing, Screenplay Based on Material from Another Medium, **John Hale, Bridget Boland**, **Richard Sokolove;** Best Cinematography, **Arthur Ibbetson;** Best Sound, **John Aldred;** Best Costume Design **Margaret Furse;** and Best Art Direction, **Maurice Carter, Lionel Couch, Patrick McLoughlin.**

For all its nominations, the only Oscar *Anne of the Thousand Days* won was Best Costume Design, which turned out to be the only Academy Award Margaret Furse ever received.

Hal Wallis was actually competing with himself that season. His film *True Grit* was up against *Anne of the Thousand Days* in several categories including Best Actor and perhaps more surprising than the fact that Richard Burton never won an Oscar is that he was beat out by none other than John Wayne, someone considered to be much more a screen personality than a serious actor. To put things in perspective, Wayne also defeated acclaimed actors Dustin Hoffman, Peter O'Toole and Jon Voigt, who were the other nominees in that category. It would seem that the Academy was more focused on sentiment than great acting in 1970.

When Richard, a six-time nominee, failed to take home an Academy Award yet again that year, the look of disappointment on Elizabeth Taylor's face was clear to see as she stood on stage and presented the Oscar for Best Picture to *Midnight Cowboy*.

Although Richard had projected indifference as the day of the Oscar ceremony approached, it seems fairly obvious that he cared about winning and was disappointed when he lost, according to the 2010 Taylor-Burton bio *Furious Love*.

Apparently, even John Wayne, himself, didn't think he deserved to win. The night of the Oscars, he was one of the many people who dropped by Richard and Elizabeth's bungalow at the Beverly Hills Hotel. The drunken actor apologized to Richard for winning the award and thrust the statuette at Richard, saying it should belong to him.

In a sense, Richard Burton got the last laugh that evening. Despite being passed over for the coveted Oscar once again, Richard did not seem like a loser at all, as he and Elizabeth remained the center of attention. They were still the fascinating golden couple, who drew more interest at the after parties than the winners, with guests swarming around, and who the press was eager to photograph.

Richard Burton and Anthony Quayle had both been nominated for Golden Globes that year, as well, but did not win. However, the movie did better, overall, at the Golden Globes than the Oscars. It won Best Motion Picture - Drama, beating out such heavyweights as *Midnight Cowboy*, *The Prime of Miss Jean Brody*, *They Shoot Horses Don't They?*, and *Butch Cassidy and the Sundance Kid*. Geneveève Bujold won Best Actress, despite stiff competition from much better established nominees Jane Fonda and Maggie Smith. Feature film newcomer Charles Jarrott won Best Director, and the writing team won Best Screenplay.

When Geneviève accepted her Golden Globe, she gave Richard Burton credit for her performance, praising his kindness, wit and in particular his generosity. The speech creates an impression of their relationship that is in stark contrast with the picture Richard's words painted in his diary at the end of filming; just one more thing that adds credibility to the theory that those diary entries may have been a cover.

In addition to the Oscars and Golden Globes, *Anne of the Thousand Days* was also nominated for two BAFTAs in the categories of Best Art Direction and Best Costume Design, and for a Writers Guild of America award in the category of Best Drama Adapted from Another Medium.

Of all the honors bestowed on the film, one of the most prestigious was the Royal Command screening for the Queen of England. Hal Wallis in particular must have been thrilled by this event, given the fact that he was such an avid Anglophile.

Hal Wallis, Charles Jarrot and writer John Hale were soon collaborating on a sequel, 1971's *Mary, Queen of Scots,* starring Vanessa Redgrave as Mary Stuart and Glenda Jackson as Elizabeth I. Although the movie was nominated for five Oscars, it was not as enthusiastically received as its predecessor, lacking the heart and many charms that *Anne of the Thousand Days* offers. It is not well remembered today. In hindsight it seems a wise decision that Geneviève Bujold refused the title role in *Mary, Queen of Scots* even though it resulted in a lawsuit for breech of contract.

Decades after its release, *Anne of the Thousand Days* holds up very well. If anything, the movie is better loved now. When it is screened today, audiences, including those made up of young adults, tend to have a very emotional reaction. Author Susan Bordo described how a crowd intensely cheered on Anne during the Tower scene, when the film was shown at a Richard Burton film festival several years back. In an interview for *Box Office Mojo,* Geneviève Bujold recalled how captivated her granddaughter was when she took her to a screening of the film that was part of the Motion Picture Arts and Sciences series "Great to be Nominated". A sparkling gem in the genre of historical drama, *Anne of the Thousand Days* is still emotionally compelling, inspiring, entertaining and surprisingly relevant 50 years later.

Fact vs. Fiction

Anne of the Thousand Days is based on history but it is a work of fiction, so historical inaccuracies are to be expected. However, finding out that the famous tower scene, which was the climax of the story and still has audiences cheering today, did not actually happen, is disappointing, all the same. The impassioned speech that Geneviève Bujold so memorably gave in the film adaptation, in which she told off Henry and refused his offer to spare her life in exchange for an annulment that would make Elizabeth illegitimate, is profoundly inspiring.

Regardless of how you might feel about her character's decision to die in order to help ensure her daughter would be Queen of England, that courageous speech is a very effective way of restoring Anne's power; otherwise we might see her, above all else, as a victim.

The scene also underscores the best thing to come out of Henry and Anne's tumultuous relationship, the glorious reign of Elizabeth I. *Anne of the Thousand Days* could still be entertaining without this scene but it wouldn't be as meaningful or compelling.

In reality, Anne's marriage to Henry was annulled two days before her execution, so she would have been fully aware that Elizabeth stood very little chance of ever being queen, unlike the fictional Anne who is so sure that her daughter will inherit the throne and be a magnificent ruler.

Although there is no indication that Henry visited Anne in the Tower after her arrest, there are hints that he may have offered her a deal to save her life. One piece of evidence comes from Anne herself, in a letter she wrote to the King, insisting on the innocence of herself and the men charged. In this letter, which Henry may have never actually seen, she seems to reference some deal that he has proposed.

According to Susan Bordo's 2013 book, *The Creation of Anne Boleyn: A New look at England's Most Notorious Queen,* Anne was hopeful that her life would be spared following a visit from Cranmer on May 16, in which she might have been offered the chance to save herself from the scaffold and live out her days in a nunnery if she admitted that her marriage and Princess Elizabeth were both illegitimate.

Her former love, Lord Percy, had denied the existence of a pre-contract with Anne, which could have been grounds for an annulment of her marriage to Henry. Therefore, Cranmer was trying to get Anne to admit that, prior to her marriage, she was aware of Henry's affair with her sister Mary. Such an admission could serve as an impediment to the lawfulness of Henry and Anne's marriage.

There is no proof that she was offered a deal by Cranmer or anyone else, but Kingston's report of Anne's cheerfulness and optimism after his visit, are a good indication that he gave her some reason to hope her sentence would be commuted if she cooperated.

Another liberty taken in the play and subsequently the screen adaptation of *Anne of the Thousand Days* is in saying that Mary Boleyn and Henry had a child together. Despite persistent rumors that Henry fathered possibly two of the children Mary Boleyn gave birth to during her marriage to William Carey, there is no proof of this.

Anne Boleyn as a Pop Culture Icon

In today's world it is difficult for a celebrity or public figure to hold the public's attention for more than a short time. It really means a lot for someone who died nearly 500 years ago to be more popular than ever. Our fascination with Anne Boleyn has never really gone away, over the centuries, although the way we perceive her has definitely evolved in certain respects.

When you think about it, Anne's pop culture icon status makes sense, especially in the 21st century, because she possessed many of the qualities than are encouraged and celebrated in modern young women. However, in Anne's own time, traits like independence, assertiveness, intellectual curiosity, strength, ambition, daring and individuality were seen as unattractive in a woman, which makes her all the more compelling to us, because she was brave enough to defy convention instead of trying to fit into a 16th century mold of the ideal woman.

Her refusal to conform probably contributed to her early demise but if she hadn't had the courage to be herself, Anne's legacy would not be what it is today. She would not continue to be so relevant, intriguing and provocative.

Media, in its many forms, has generated more interest in Anne Boleyn than ever. Books, movies, plays, TV, the internet, have all contributed to her ascension to superstardom. Susan Bordo's thorough and insightful book, *The Creation of Anne Boleyn: A New Look at England's Most Notorious Queen*, sheds light on the real woman, while also exploring her pop culture persona and the impact she's had on society through the years. According to Bordo, Anne has been a source of inspiration for many young women, who see her as a role model. Bordo explains how projects like Showtime's *The Tudors* have driven her fame and popularity among younger generations.

The many faces of Anne are also beneficial to her longevity in the public eye. Some celebrities prolong their marketability by constantly reinventing themselves. Historians, literature, and the media have done this for Anne. We don't tire of her as easily as some historical figures because she has been projected in a number of different ways, ranging from near saint to treacherous siren. We have seen the virtuous, misunderstood scapegoat, the sophisticated intellectual who was too clever for her own good, the seductress so potent she could give Delilah and Aphrodite a run for their money and of course, the scheming, malevolent opportunist. The fact that we don't know, for sure, which of these, or more likely which combination, comes closest to describing the real Anne, makes her even more interesting.

Anne Boleyn has actually been part of pop culture for a very long time, beginning with romantic novels, which fictionalized her life, as well as stage plays and films, even the opera.

Authors have been writing about Anne for over four hundred years including historians and fiction writers, which have sometimes been one and the same. A major source of material for both fiction and nonfiction centering on Anne Boleyn, over the years, are the letters of Spanish Ambassador Eustace Chapuys, who was clearly very biased against her and gloried in her downfall. It is mainly from these slanderous letters that we get the conniving, she-devil image of Anne.

In theologian and reformer Alexander Ales' letter to her daughter, Elizabeth I, reminiscing about Anne, the virtuous woman of conviction he paints could not be more opposite from the image of Anne that Chapuy's described. Ales also gave

Anne substantial credit for establishing the Protestant religion in England as did John Foxe in one of his pro-Anne books, *The Acts and Monuments of the Church* (also known as *The Book of Martyrs*), published in 1563, in which he highly praised her character.

The main reason Anne has been such a polarizing figure is because of differences in religious ideology. Traditionally, Catholics viewed her as a villainous heretic while Protestants often saw her as a hero, even a saint. Much of what we read about her, even today, is rooted in these two opposing precepts; although both religions agree on the major impact she had in the Reformation, which is probably why their feelings toward her tend to be so extreme one way or the other.

Nicholas Sander's sensationalistic 1585 book *Schismatis Anglicani* (*The Rise and Growth of the Anglican Schism*), later adapted into a school play, has been a powerful and far-reaching indictment on Anne from the fervent Catholic sector. Anne's reputation as a manipulative seductress can be largely traced to this book.

Writers like George Wyatt, who wrote a favorable biography of Anne and defended her against Sander's accusations, and George Cavendish, who maligned her in his biography of Cardinal Wolsey, kept the debate about the controversial queen going, over the next century.

Playwrights have long been inspired by Anne's story, an ideal theatrical vehicle. John Banks' very popular 1682 play *Virtue Betray'd* also called *Anna Bullen*, full of palace intrigues, Catholic conspiracy and melodrama, casts Anne as a sympathetic victim.

William Shakespeare, who was greatly patronized by Elizabeth I and wrote plays that were sympathetic to the Tudors, presented an Anne in *The Famous History of the Life of King Henry the Eighth*, who wanted to be loyal to Katherine and was practically dragged onto the throne against her will, deeply contrasting with the frequent depiction of her as an ambitious opportunist.

The play, which is one of Shakespeare's lesser works, might have been better received if he had developed Anne's character, but it may have been that Shakespeare shied away from fleshing her out, which probably would have meant making her more human and exposing flaws. Considering she was the mother of his benefactress, he could have easily felt obligated to portray Anne in the most flattering light even though Elizabeth had been dead for 10 years by the time the play was first produced in 1613.

Like Shakespeare's Anne, in the version of her from Tom Taylor's successful 1875 play, Anne sympathizes with Queen Katherine and regrets taking her place. Whether the real Anne pitied Katherine or felt any true remorse over the part she had in the Queen's downfall, may remain unclear to us, but it's easier for audiences to support the Other Woman when she is reluctant and subsequently contrite for her actions.

Gaetano Donizetti's beloved *Anna Bolena* was first performed in 1830. It was one of four Tudor era operas Donizetti composed, three of which were about queens. Set in 1536, *Anna Bolena* covers the period between the breakdown of Anne and Henry's relationship and her execution. This opera has continued to be popular and has starred such iconic divas as Maria Callas and Beverly Sills.

One of the first writers to novelize Anne's story was Marie Catherine Le Jumel de Barneville, also known by her pseudonym Madame d'Aulnoy. This author, who is sometimes credited with inventing the fairytale genre – originally created for adults-- wrote a story focusing on Anne Boleyn in the late 17th century. She was well-suited to write a book such as this because, like Anne herself, d'Aulnoy was ahead of her time. The author frequently wrote about smart, resourceful young women who are being ill-treated by paternal authority figures. The book she wrote titled: *The Novels of Elizabeth, Queen of England, Containing the History of Queen Anne of Bullen*, was much more about Anne than her daughter Elizabeth and is not unlike a dark fairytale. Making Anne the protagonist of a story like this was innovative because there weren't really any tragic female heroines in literature at the time.

A young Jane Austen was inspired by Anne Boleyn, praising and defending her, as she adamantly denounces Henry VIII, in *The History of England*, which Austen composed in 1791, when she was just 16-years-old. Many years after Austen's school girl musings, came another passionate defense of Anne, her 1821 biography by Elizabeth Benger titled *Memoirs of the Life of Anne Boleyn*. She gives Anne a great deal of credit for the Reformation and rejects the image of her as power-seeking seductress. Benger is probably the first author to explore the issue of gender expectations in an analysis of Anne and Henry's relationship.

Anne Boleyn has been a popular subject of novels from the early 20th century onward. *The Favor of Kings* (1912) by Mary Hastings Bradley is a well-researched novel which showed candor for its time, depicting a pre-marital sexual relationship between Henry and Anne. Instead of either demonizing or canonizing her, as authors were apt to do, Bradley wanted to humanize Anne, which she did in her relatively identifiable depiction of her as a vulnerable youth, while attempting to delve into a youthful Anne's psyche and present her story from a very personal perspective.

During the freewheeling 1920s Anne Boleyn was particularly relatable to the daring, spirited, somewhat liberated young women known as flappers, and this side of her personality was played up in literature. It was also during this era that descriptions and artistic rendering of her physical appearance, i.e. slender figure and dark complexion, became more accurate as these features were now more fashionable.

Anne continued to be a sympathetic and likable figure in most literary representations for many years but, as the very wholesome 1950s approached, one of the most famous novels about the disgraced queen, Margaret Campbell Barnes' salacious 1949 book, *Brief Gaudy Hour: A Novel of Anne Boleyn*, resurrected her image as a skillful sexual manipulator and opportunist.

It's not surprising that moviemakers were quick to adapt the story of Henry VIII and Anne Boleyn. One early motion picture, focusing specifically on Anne, was the 1920 silent movie by highly regarded filmmaker Ernst Lubitsch, in which she was played by Henny Porten. The captivating production with its vivid characterizations lives up to its tagline: "The real heart story of Anne Boleyn".

The exotically beautiful and sensual Merle Oberon played Anne Boleyn in memorable 1933 dramedy biopic *The Private Lives of Henry VIII*, which chronicles the King's last five marriages and features Charles Laughton's cartoonish but iconic portrayal of Henry VIII.

Joyce Redman's feisty heroine in *Anne of the Thousand Days* was a hit with theater-goers but Maxwell Anderson's frank and passionate retelling of "The King's Great Matter" would not be deemed appropriate for the cinema until a new generation had come of age. However, in late 1969 when edginess and realism in movies were all the rage, *Anne of the Thousand Days,* despite the scandalous subject matter, was not as enthusiastically received as it likely would have been several years earlier.

The glamorous, elegant production which, in many respects, harkens back to the Golden Age of Hollywood, inspired mixed reviews. But one thing most critics could agree on was that Geneviève Bujold gave an excellent performance. Watching the production today, it's her embodiment of Anne that stands out most and continues to captivate us.

After researching Anne, in preparation for the role, Geneviève had a joyful and energetic attitude toward the woman she was portraying, due in part to Anne's independence, and her sense of self, two qualities that vividly come through in her performance. Geneviève's Anne was timely for the late 1960s and could resonate with feminists.

The actress helped to separate Anne from the deeply disparaging, sexist propaganda that had compromised her reputation during her life and long after her death. Working within Max Anderson's characterization, she helped to replace the image of Anne as a scheming harlot, who sexually manipulated her way to the throne, with a strong, brave, dignified and likable woman who we could admire in many respects.

 Geneviève's depiction of Anne Boleyn might very well be the most beloved and compelling of all time, but these things are subjective and there have been other actresses who were very popular in the role. Decades after *Anne of the Thousand Days*, in an interview with author Susan Bordo, Geneviève Bujold found it impossible to name a contemporary actress she would choose to play Anne, or who would do the character justice, reluctantly admitting she felt the part belonged to her. Many of her fans feel the same way.

The talented Philippa Gregory, who has written several entertaining historical novels set at the Tudor Court, was partially responsible for a resurgence of interest in Anne Boleyn during the first decade of the 2000s, with her juicy read *The Other Boleyn Girl*, which was released in 2001 and became a big commercial and critical success. However, some critics have found considerable fault with the book due to what could be viewed as significant historical inaccuracies. Of course, it's called historical fiction for a reason -- we have to expect liberties to be taken -- but Gregory's novels are held to a different standard because she has repeatedly talked about the importance she places on historical accuracy when she writes this kind of book.

In addition to events found in *The Other Boleyn Girl* that are derived from rumor, or invented by Philippa Gregory, some readers are troubled by her characterization of Anne, which revives the ruthless, manipulative predatory vixen depicted in old Catholic propaganda and in the letters of her enemy Ambassador Chapuys.

The image of Anne Boleyn has come a long way over the years. In the 20th century an alternate view of her began to take hold. Instead of always being perceived as either a one dimensional villain or a helpless victim, she was celebrated in some works as a brave, spirited, intelligent, liberated woman, unfairly slandered and misunderstood in her own time, who is worthy of admiration and respect. Gregory's focus on Anne's much contested bad girl persona, threatened to undermine her as someone who could actually be a positive role model.

The 2008 film adaptation of *The Other Boleyn Girl*, written by Philippa Gregory and Peter Morgan, goes even further in making Anne out to be a despicable, unsympathetic viper. It is no wonder that Natalie Portman, who portrayed her in the film, could not relate to the character. It's likely that the majority of moviegoers felt the same way. But where this version of Anne may have failed to inspire young women, the incarnation of her played by Natalie Dormer in Showtime series *The Tudors*, succeeded. The real life admiration and emotional connection Dormer felt for Anne was undoubtedly part of what made her performance so powerful.

Dormer, who is well informed when it comes to history, struggled to ensure Anne was portrayed as accurately as possible. When she auditioned for the role with her natural hair color, blonde, Dormer assumed that if she was cast, she would have to dye it, which is exactly what she did as soon as she was notified that she had the part, only to find out producers had planned for her to play Anne Boleyn as a blonde.

The Showtime executives were very unhappy about her becoming a brunette, and she feared they would make her wear a blonde wig for the role. It wasn't just a matter of being historically accurate. Dormer felt it was important to play Anne dark because it was something that contrasted with the ideal of beauty in 16th century England. However, Anne was noticeably self-assured despite her unfashionably dark hair and complexion. Dormer explained her feelings to the cable network's president of entertainment, Bob Greenblatt, who eventually agreed to let her play the role as a brunette.

Sex was a major part of *The Tudors* and the main reason Dormer got the role was because of the chemistry she had with Jonathan Rhys Meyers, who was cast as Henry, but as it turned out, Dormer made a much bigger contribution to the series than onscreen sparks with her leading man. As a champion of Anne Boleyn, Dormer was distressed over the show's practice of recycling negative sensationalistic stereotypes, which pigeon holed her as the classic Other Woman during the first season of the show.

The more positive way in which Anne was presented in *The Tudors* second season was due in large part to input from Dormer herself, who convinced the creator/writer of the series, Michael Hirst, to be more fair is his depiction of her. The sensual character was suddenly equipped with an impressive intellect, political savvy and was seriously dedicated to the Reformist cause. Her maternal side, something that is greatly overshadowed by other aspects of her persona, was also displayed.

The fact that we readily buy into the stereotype of Anne as a calculating home-wrecking whore, and that so many authors have gotten away with portraying her as such, based apparently on very biased sources or highly dubious evidence, says a lot about the prevalence of sexist attitudes in our culture. But by the same token, the popularity of an alternate version, Anne the heroine, which has been gaining strength, at least since the mid-20th century, indicates the progress we have made toward tearing down sexual stereotypes.

Anne is more relatable than the typical feminist icon, in part because she is refreshingly human and her flaws are so front and center. She is also more intriguing than many of the women who are held up as serious role models for 21st century females.

One of Anne's most endearing qualities and which, along with her spirit and independence help her to be a relevant pop culture icon for the modern era, is her often wry sense of humor

Anne Boleyn's notable wit was a part of her charm and helps us to relate to her today. It is especially impressive how she was able to hold on to her sense of humor at even the most daunting of times. After being arrested and taken to the

Tower, Anne asked Constable Kingston if she was going to die without justice, and despite her intense anxiety at the time, she had to laugh out loud in response to Kingston's assurance that even the poorest of the King's subjects had justice.

Her humor also came out during the trial when witnesses testified to remarks she and her brother George made, mocking Henry's poetry and wardrobe. The most famous example of her wit was shortly before her execution, when she implied that her tiny neck should make the beheading easier.

Our interest in Anne continues today with books, plays, movies and TV series about or prominently featuring this controversial queen, who has proven to be one of the most culturally enduring historical figures of all time. A simple explanation that most fans and critics of Anne would accept is that she was a colorful, daring woman, progressive in her thinking and behavior, who was significantly responsible for bringing about monumental change in society through her part in the religious Reformation. Her multifaceted legacy entertains, inspires, and to some extent shapes our world in a much broader sense. Therefore, our fascination with Anne Boleyn thrives perhaps eternally.

Selected Bibliography

Books, Periodicals, and Websites

Adams, James. "Geneviève Bujold at 70: 'I'm Free in Front of the Camera.'" *The Globe and Mail*. Published May 2, 2013. Updated May 11, 2018. https://www.theglobeandmail.com/arts/film/genevieve-bujold-at-70-im-free-in-front-of-the-camera/article11680566/

Anderson, Hesper. *South Mountain Road: A Daughter's Journey of Discovery*. New York: Simon & Schuster. 2000.

Anderson, Maxwell. *Anne of the Thousand Days*. New York: Dramatists Play Services, Inc. 1977.

The Anne Boleyn Files. https://www.theanneboleynfiles.com/category/the-tudors/

Bell, Joseph, N. "Geneviève Bujold: A Rising Star." *The Montreal Gazette*. June 19, 1970. https://news.google.com/newspapers?id=2osyAAAAIBAJ&sjid=IbkFAAAAIBAJ&pg=1134,4849351&dq=she-didnt-really-enjoy-anne-the-first-time&hl=en

Benger, Elizabeth. *Memoirs of the Life of Anne Boleyn, Queen of King Henry VIII*. London: A. & R. Spottiswoode, 1821.

Bordo, Susan. *The Creation of Anne Boleyn: A New look at England's Most Notorious Queen*. Boston and New York: Houghton Mifflin Harcourt, 2013.

Burton, Richard, edited by Williams, Chris. *The Richard Burton Diaries*. New Haven and London: Yale University Press, 2012.

Carradice, Phil. "The Death of Richard Burton." *BBC*. August 5, 2014. https://www.bbc.co.uk/blogs/wales/entries/ce7834d3-1e40-3389-855a-02392d9c0549

"Cinema: The Lion in Autumn." *Time*. February 2, 1970. http://content.time.com/time/magazine/article/0,9171,878191,00.html

Collins, Glenn. "Sir Anthony Quayle, British Actor And Theater Director, Dies at 76." *The New York Times*. Oct. 21, 1989. https://www.nytimes.com/1989/10/21/obituaries/sir-anthony-quayle-british-actor-and-theater-director-dies-at-76.html

Dowd, Maureen. "Richard Burton, 58, is Dead; Rakish Stage and Screen Star." August 6, 1984. *The New York Times*. http://movies2.nytimes.com/learning/general/onthisday/bday/1110.html

Ebert, Roger. "Interview with Irene Papas." ROGEREBERT.com. July 13. 1969. https://www.rogerebert.com/interviews/interview-with-irene-papas

Foxe, John. *The Acts and Monuments of John Foxe*. The Church Historians of England. Vol. V. London: Beeleys, 1857.

Georges Delerue Official Website. http://www.georges-delerue.com/

Gregory, Philippa. *The Other Boleyn Girl*. New York: Pocket Star Books, 2007.

Holleran, Scott. "Close-Up: Actress Genevieve Bujold." *Box Office Mojo*. April 13, 2007. https://www.boxofficemojo.com/features/?id=2290&p=.htm

IBDB. Anne of the Thousand Days. https://www.ibdb.com/broadway-show/anne-of-the-thousand-days-1612

Ives, Eric. *The Life and Death of Anne Boleyn*. Malden, MA: Blackwell Publishing, 2005.

Kashner, Sam, and Schoenberger, Nancy. *Furious Love: Elizabeth Taylor, Richard Burton, and the Marriage of the Century*. New York: It Books, 2011.

Klein, Alvin. "Keeping Alive the Works of Maxwell Anderson." *The New York Times*. May 3, 1998. https://www.nytimes.com/1998/05/03/nyregion/keeping-alive-the-work-of-maxwell-anderson.html

Loades, David. *The Six Wives of Henry VIII*. Gloucestershire, UK: Amberley Publishing Plc, 2009.

Maxwell, Robin. *Mademoiselle Boleyn*. New York: New American Library, 2007.

Mowis, I.S. "Anthony Quayle Mini Bio." *IMDB*. https://www.imdb.com/name/nm0703033/bio?ref_=nm_ov_bio_sm

Mullin, Michael. *Design by Motley*. Newark: University of Delaware Press. London: Associated University Presses, 1996.

Sander, Nicholas. The *Rise and Growth of the Anglican Schism*: London: Burns and Oates, 1877.

Shepherd, Melinda, C. "Charles Jarrott, British Director." *Encyclopedia Britannica* https://www.britannica.com/biography/Charles-Jarrott.

Shivers, Alfred, S. *The Life of Maxwell Anderson*, New York: Stein and Day, 1983.

Stein, Sadie. "A Journey of Discovery." *The Paris Review*. September 4, 2015. https://www.theparisreview.org/blog/2015/09/04/a-journey-of-discovery/

Wallis, Hal, and Higham, Charles. *Starmaker: The Autobiography of Hal Wallis*. New York: Macmillan Publishing CO. INC., 1980.

Windeler, Robert. "I'm Insecure but Strong." *People*. March 20, 1978. https://people.com/archive/cover-story-im-insecure-but-strong-vol-9-no-11/

Weir, Alison. *Elizabeth of York: A Tudor Queen and Her World*, New York: Ballantine Books, 2014.

Visual Material
Interviews and documentary footage

Behind the scenes on the Production of 'Anne of the Thousand Days. 1969, filming at Hever Castle with interviews with Geneviève Bujold, Hal Wallis, Richard Burton. Filming with Anthony Quayle. Storyboards and costumes. Huntley Film Archives, film no 227.

The Carolyn Jackson Collection, no 58 - Interview with Charles Jarrott. 1977.

The Dick Cavett Show. Richard Burton: Part 1 and 2. 1980.

Michael Parkinson's Interview with Richard Burton, November 23, 1974, BFI Archive.

Feature Films and Television Dramatizations

Anne of the Thousand Days; Becket; Casablanca; Circle of Two; Cleopatra; King of Hearts; Mary, Queen of Scots; My Cousin Rachel; My Fair Lady; Murder by Decree; The Other Boleyn Girl; Poor Little Rich Girl: The Barbara Hutton Story; The Rainmaker; The Shadow of the Tower; The Spy Who Came in from the Cold; The Taming of the Shrew; The Tudors; Tom Jones; Who's Afraid of Virginia Woolf?

Printed in Great Britain
by Amazon